THE AMATEUR

2nd Edition

THE AMATEUR - 2ND EDITION

The Amateur - 2nd Edition is the first part of the series Brushes & Mouses written by Felipe Reis, Phillip Reese or J.F. Reis.

It was finished in December 2022 and revised in May 2026.

This book is available on Amazon websites with the same name followed by the country code.

Please note that Amazon Spain serves Portugal.

All images, titles, subtitles and texts associated with the authors Felipe Reis, Phillip Reese and J.F. Reis are copyrighted.

No part of this book may be reproduced in any form or by any means without the prior approval of the author.

A good part of the works have been published by
https://www.artmajeur.com/phillip-reese

ISBN: 9798369974902

THE AMATEUR - 2ND EDITION
As in December 2022

BRUSHES & MICE is the book following *THE AMATEUR - 2ND EDITION*
while *O AMADOR* and *PINCEIS E RATOS* are their editions in Portuguese.

Other books by the author:

BEFORE I LOST MY COUNTRY published in English on Amazon,
was translated into Portuguese with the title *1974*.

I AM A WOMAN, I AM by JF Reis is available on Amazon.
Its translation, *SOU MULHER, EU SOU* by JF Reis, is available on Amazon Sp.

A condensed version has the name of *POEMS RIDING POEMS* by PHILLIP REESE.

BREXIT NEWS: A POT STEW WITH MAY, BORIS, SHOES, AND SAILS by
Phillip Reese is a book of images and sub-titles about Teresa May
up to the moment Boris Johnson tries to come of age.

Other books:

BIRDS and SQUIRRELS, PASSARINHOS E ESQUILOS,
OCTOBER 2025 (art), BOBBING WINGS and
BUBBLES OF LIFE (kind of words post my accident), ALIENS and : art, comment, stories
(also, after my accident to be sure I could do something,
all repeated but one work, unpublished now, I think),
JON, BOLT, Faísca, João, memories of a young life,
English and Portuguese, some still being revised,
THE EXOTIS, The Not Successful submission to the TATE MODERN;
Destiny Building Site, Ultimate Love,
WHO AM I? (for my grand-children),
THE TIMES ART CAPSULE (all pictures from the work in acrylic) ;

Notice

All the frames of the paintings published in this book,
were created and handmade by the author
for the exhibition "LIKE DON'T LIKE".

Dedication

My ideas are richer than my artistic creations,
may both remain in harmony.

I dedicate this book to Rodica.
Our 28-year friendship has so far survived
many lively periods in both our lives.

*

The images on the front and back cover
are some of the hundreds of images in the books

BRUSHES & MICE, MICE & BRUSHES
and a few others published more recently.

Preamble

From darkness to lightness.

I used art, short poems and mobile phone messages to make sense of my new world outside troubled Angola, but also of my long and difficult life.

This was definitely a healing process – the beginning of a long journey towards liberation from a harsh but not entirely innocent past because I was the odd guy. No one could understand me and me them.

The book discusses all my paintings on canvas one by one, explaining why I created them and how each one took me a step further towards sanity and adaptation to life in the UK.

The second edition of The Amateur, revised now in 2026, contains a few more acrylic and digital paintings than the first edition. I make no excuses for the quality of my paintings and images. For me, creating them was simply a challenge that helped me find balance in my life. That's what makes them so personally valuable.

Many people can have that experience. For me, painting alone was not enough; I also had to write about it. This worked because each time I opened an unsettled compartment of my past life, I closed it again.

The book Brushes & Mice and others are free from the thorns of the past. Nevertheless, it is the first sequel to The Amateur and part of the same series.

Brushes & Mice and Mice & Brushes contain lighter and funnier images and stories based on my alien friends, The Exotis, stories that I was previously not capable of producing - a good sign.

My late books depict better images, I think.

Phillip Reese

London, December 2022

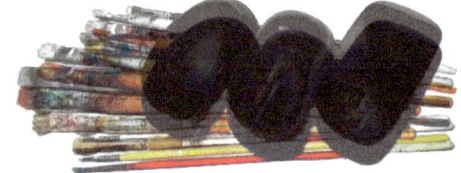

Table of contents

PART I - Beginnings 9
    The Art Exhibition LIKE DON'T LIKE (2012) 9
    Paintings (2005-2014) 10
    The Flight of the Three Graces Saving the Last Green on Earth (2005) 10
    THE TIMES Art Capsule or The Time Art Capsule (2005-2006) 11
    The Blue Shell (2006) 12
    Xmas 2006 13
    The Last Fire on Earth (2008) 13
    Rodica's Portrait (2007) 14
    Calm Before the Storm: Earth, Water, Air and Fire (2008) 15
    The Painting with no name (2008) 15
    Hope and Freedom (2008) 16
    The Ovary (2008) 17
    The Olympic Bronze Medal (2008) 17
    The Twelve Gordins, or The Twelve Apost'rophes of the 2008-09 Credit Crunch Greedy Gang ... 18
    The Twelve Gordins Pamphlet 19
    Madonna and Child (1975-2010) 19
    The First Wrinkle and Botox (2010) 21
    The Ghost of the Eight O'clock Goodbye (2008) 22
    The Gates of Hell (2011) - Les Portes de L'Enfer Vivant 22
    Homeless 23
    Dream of Lightness 24
    The Muse 24
    The Four Civil Servants Values (February 2011) 25
    The Former Copperways Hotel 26
    History of Portugal on the flag 26
    Thomas Hewlett House 28
    Waterspout on a Beautiful Day (2015) 28
    Two Faces (2015) 29
    Diving into the Olympics (2016) 29
    Columbo's Migrants Flying Machine (2018) 30

Illustrations made for my poems - The Transition 32
    Rodica told me her story 35
    Digital Transformations (pre-2014) and facing the computer 36

Learning and discovering. 38
    2013 40
    Each little square contains a photo. 40

Thomas Hewlett House, again. 41
    This book is being revised at the moment 47

Part II 48
    Next are a few little pieces of art out 48
    of the hundreds I did, ... 48
    some of which are recent (2026). 48

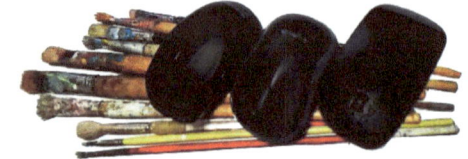

PART I - Beginnings

Gayton Road

*

The Art Exhibition LIKE DON'T LIKE (2012)

My life in London was once interrupted when my car was vandalised. It turned out that the culprits were two neighbours who had recently arrived in the country. Feeling in danger, I retreated into my survival cocoon. Under duress, I built a garage that could accommodate two large cars, as well as serving as a studio and workshop. It was very expensive, but safety was my top priority.

Having recently retired, I needed to justify this decision by proving that I could build a 12-by-5-metre structure. I succeeded — I did it on my own. I then used this space to exhibit the artworks I had created up to that point. To enrich the event artistically, I created an art installation called 'Shoe Story'.

The story is simple: a man and a woman marry and have a daughter. The man has an affair with a woman he meets at a tennis club, and the couple divorce. This narrative is conveyed through a simple

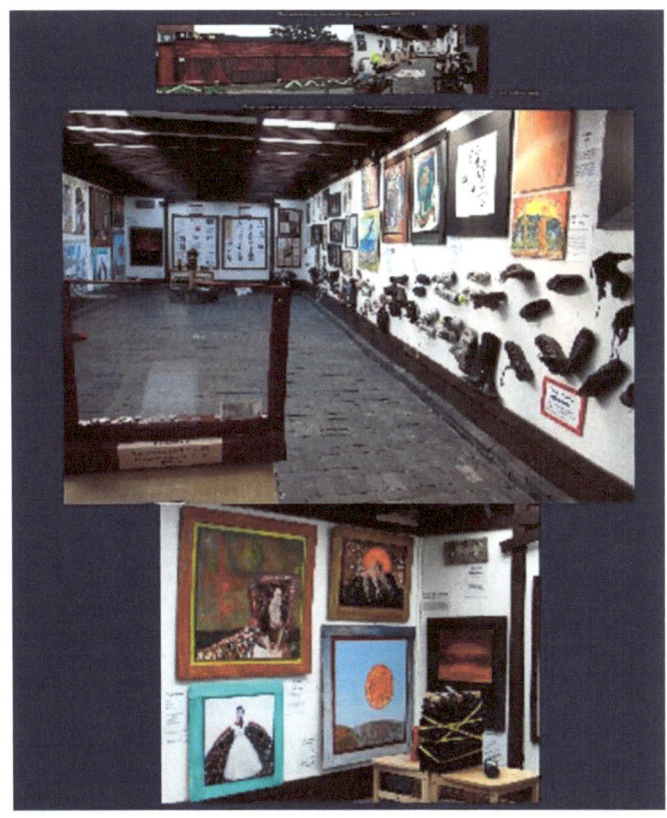

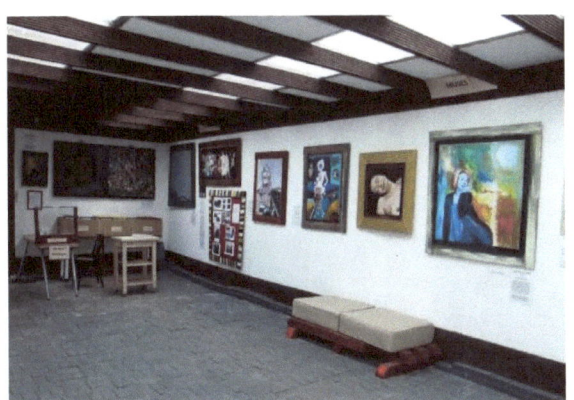

arrangement of shoes mounted on a wall.

A week later, Harrow Council in London ordered me to take down this building and exhibition. I did it! It was fun to burn it all down, piece by piece, after I had enjoyed my exhibition. Thankfully, the works of art and poems survived.

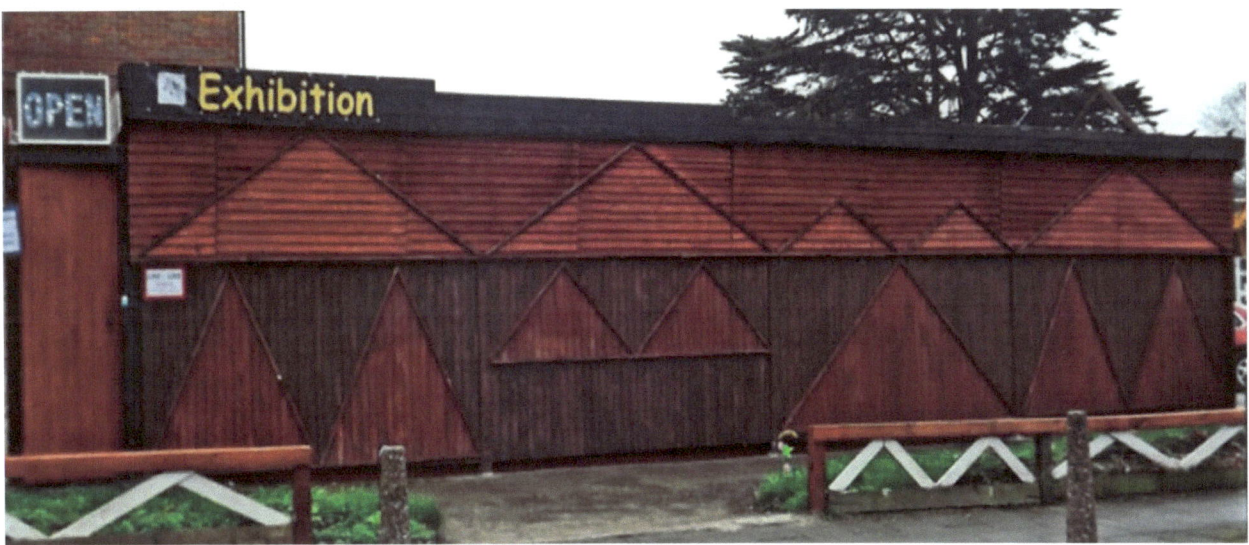

Pinner Road

Paintings (2005-2014)

*

The Flight of the Three Graces Saving the Last Green on Earth (2005)

The Scorched Earth series began with this work. It was painted in acrylic on a 30"x20" canvas.

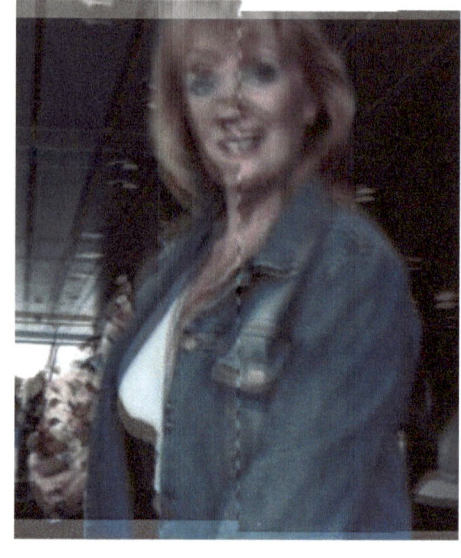

Jean, an independent and confident woman, invited me to visit her. Even before I met her in person, she had been my first muse. The short poems I wrote for her, all in English, were the first tools I used to challenge the prejudices and preconceived ideas that had dominated my past. This experience made me want to adapt to life in the country.

At her rented house on a canal in the Midlands, I finally realised an idea I had held for some time: I used charcoal to do a drawing on white paper. Upon returning to London, I began working on my first ever painting in acrylic, 'The Three Graces'. When I had finished it, I hung it on one of the blank grey walls in the flat I was renting.

This painting shows how little I knew about painting, for ex. using white paint to represent light and shadows. Looking at it now, it's also clear how little I knew about the human body.

However, Jean gave me the courage to change my approach to life, and this painting marks the beginning of my discovery of who I am.

The Three Graces embody not only the familiar concept of female sisterhood. They convey the idea that the land, which we share with small viruses, bacteria, trees, algae and plankton, as well as 'higher' organisms such as dogs, cats and humans, should be destroyed by natural phenomena, rather than by human intervention.

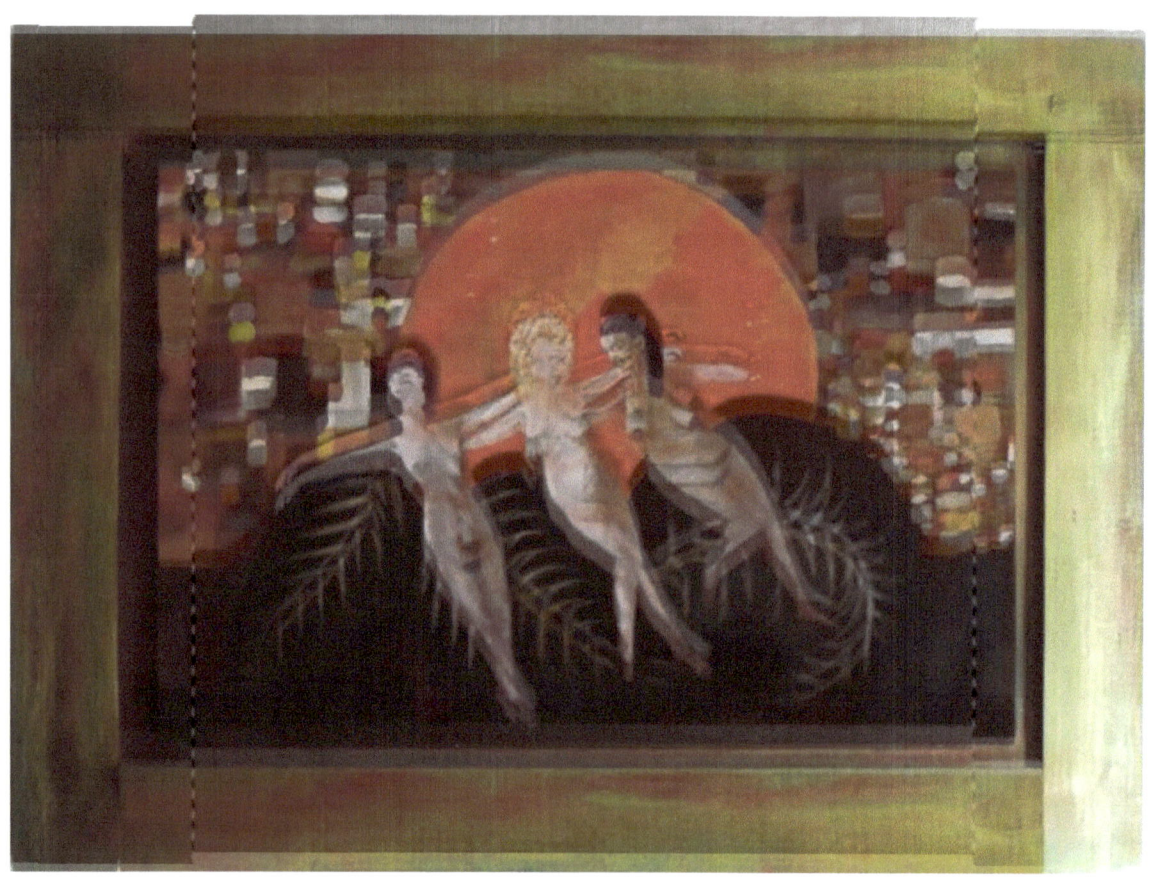

THE TIMES' Art Capsule or The Time Art Capsule (2005-2006)

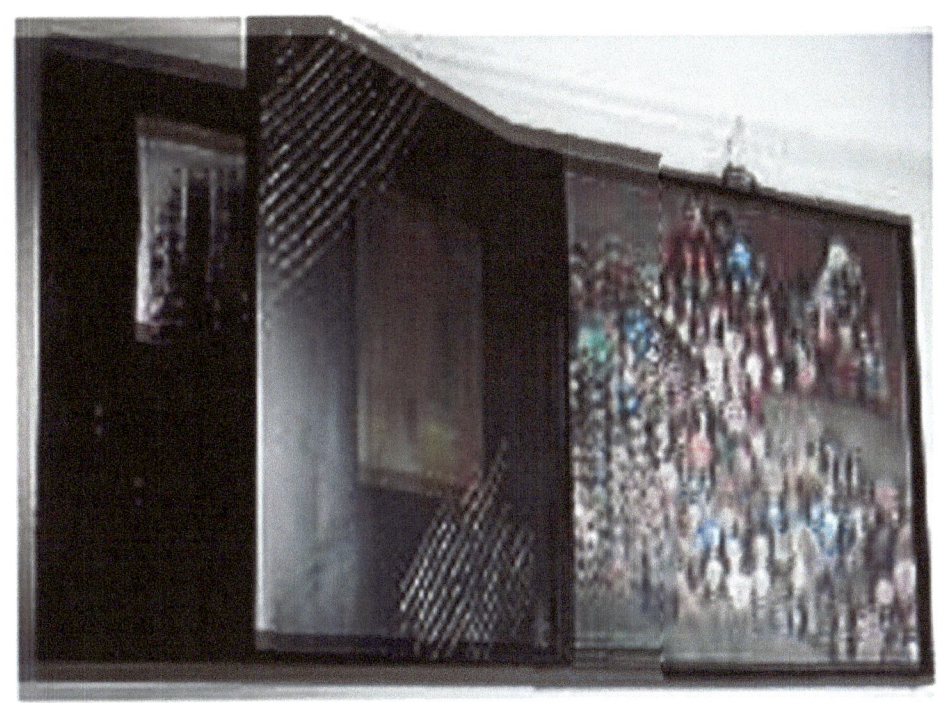

It is an installation consisting of a box that opens like a book, displaying two 80 x 90 cm canvases side by side. They are painted in acrylic, with the canvas on the left opening like a page from a book.

Hidden on the back of this canvas are the brushes I used to paint it, the tooth I lost during the five months it took me to complete the installation and a copy of the 20 October 2005 edition of the London newspaper, The Times, which featured the 254 faces I painted on the canvas.

Visible in the photo are also two padlocks that secure the installation when the box is closed.

I created this piece to practise using colour, but when I started painting the faces, I realised that I was also creating news, the work itself, like a newspaper columnist does.

Professionals write about facts as truthfully as their status demands, but it is impossible to avoid adding a little extra 'colour' to the characters of the chosen topic.

For this reason, I painted a typical portrait of each professional, while all the other faces (the subjects of news stories and adverts) were painted in many colours.

The third aspect. The canvas on the left is all about 'My News' and 'My Heart News'. This phase of my life was short-lived, and even now I still don't fully understand it, but that's just how I am!

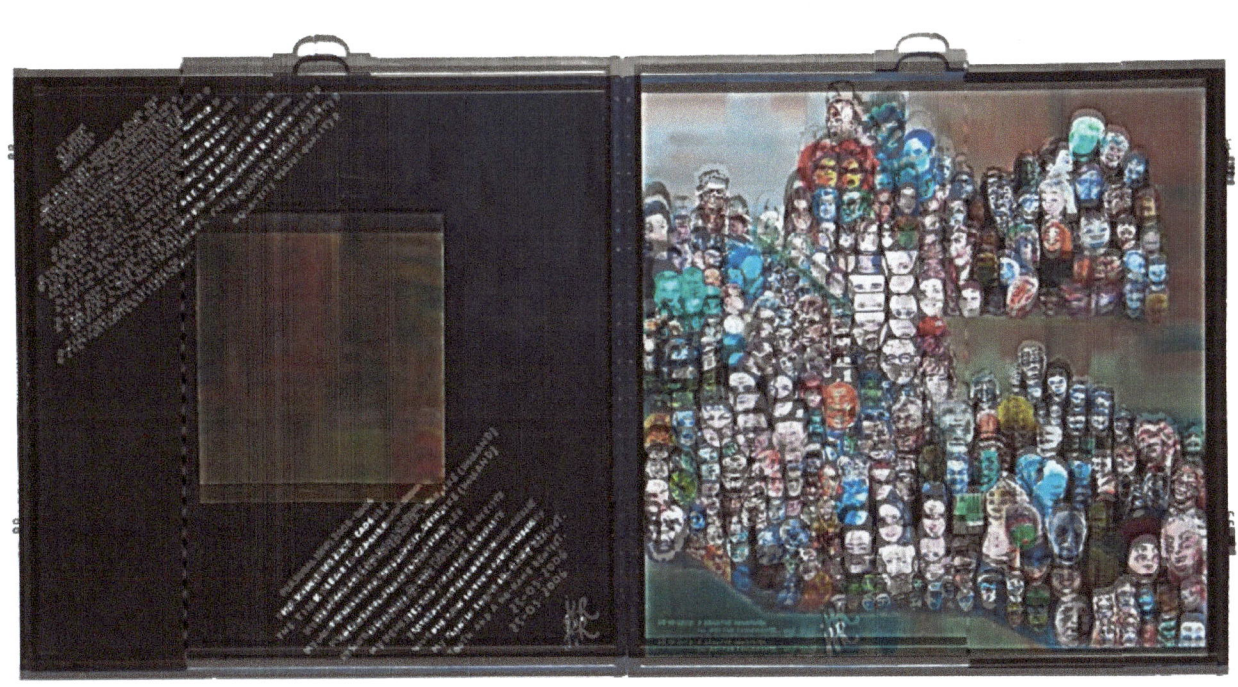

The Blue Shell (2006)
Acrylic on canvas, 90cmx90cm.

    This case received national publicity for a few weeks. I am sure that a teacher who would not educate her own children in that way would not instruct children with a veiled face. Children need to be able to read facial expressions when communicating with others, and ideally combine this with the sound of a voice. If the pupils were adults, I would see no problem with her teaching them using a veil.
    The centre of the discussion was whether the veil was a political statement, a matter of human rights, or a way for her to obey the prescriptions of her religion or culture. Furthermore, if our educational system were to accept a teacher displaying such behaviour, it would effectively be tolerating every culture in the world to come to the UK and freely express its customs.
    I used to live in Lubango in Angola, where the Mumuíla tribe live nearby. They are the most peaceful people I have ever known. Families would come to town wearing only loincloths and sometimes light cloths over their shoulders.
    If we respect all cultures in the UK, we should welcome these former neighbours of mine in London despite the way they dress — almost naked — and tolerate their natural smells (they never bathe, use animal oils to protect their skin, and use sour milk in their hairstyles).

Years ago in Portugal, Catholic women wore capes and veils, and today, Mumuílas from Angola do the same. Unfortunately, the curiosity of tourists is so great that the people of this tribe have adapted in order to satisfy onlookers. Women used to decorate their limbs and necks with heavy metal rings to indicate their social status; for example, whether they were single or married. Today, however, they wear small, colourful plastic beads. The photo shows colourful, clean clothes. They were never like that, so I assume the photographer made them wear them. History, adaptation and common sense are needed.

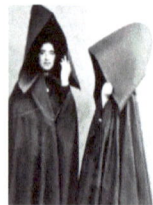 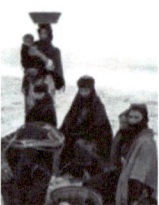 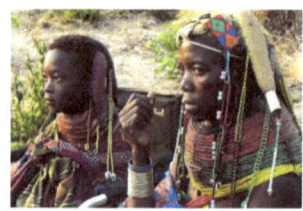

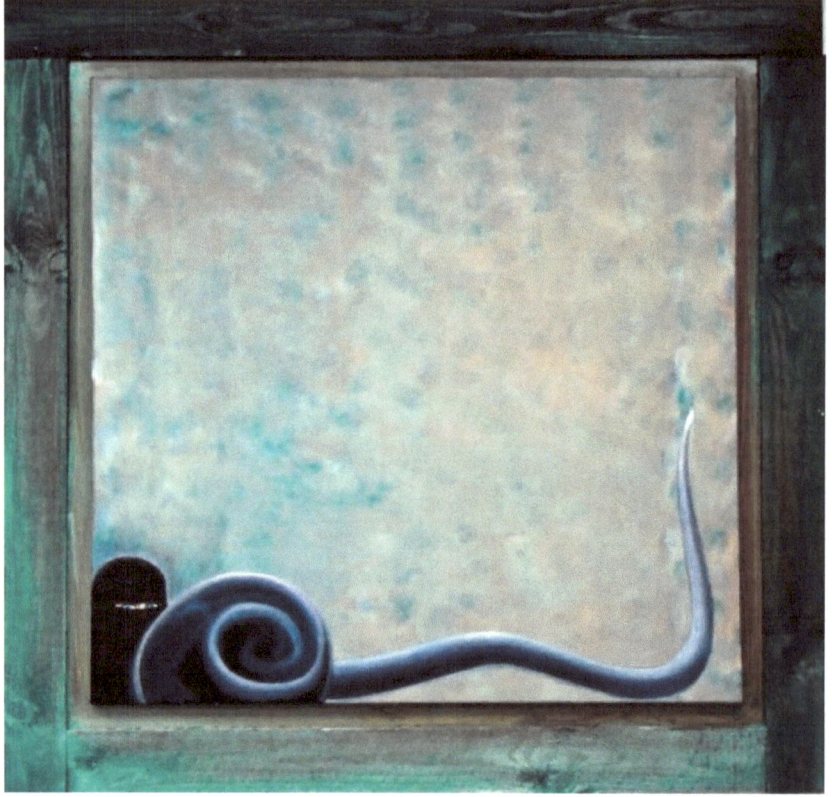

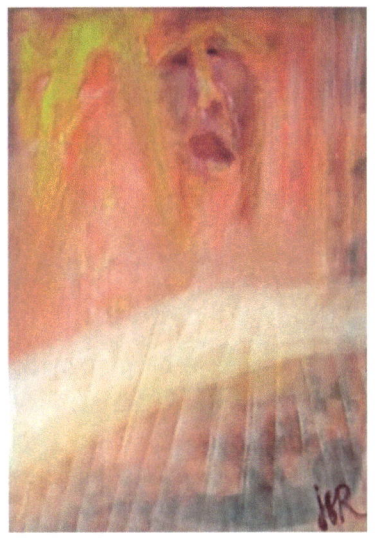

Xmas 2006
Acrylic on canvas, 30"x20".

I failed the last Advanced Databases exam. It was in January, the university had scheduled three final exams in one day - two in the morning and this, the most difficult one, in the afternoon.

I was well prepared, but that week I got ill and developed a high fever. At the time of the final exam, for some reason, my brain started producing the wrong chemicals, or they became unbalanced, causing interesting results.

I remember reading some questions and feeling very happy. They were 'very' simple, which didn't seem appropriate for such a difficult subject. I started to answer the questions. I wrote pure wisdom, synthetic poetry and the most beautiful sentences ever. My answers were magnificent. To simplify the whole process, I used logical mathematical expressions instead of answering them in English. This way, all the answers would be perfect: clear, precise and concise.

I did not realise that what I was writing was nothing more than a set of very short cryptic and completely meaningless illogical expressions. At the time, the option was simple, why to explain the diabolical intricacies of data management in English when I could do it with just a few logical symbols?

I got zero marks. I was surprised. How could I have failed? After all, I thought that exam had gone perfectly.

I didn't know the power of inner drugs, or whether they were caused by fatigue and illness. A month later, I took the resit and got 95%, although the grade didn't count (regardless of the result, the lowest pass mark would still be recorded).

Years later, I was ill again at the end of the year. This time, I was alone in bed without food. I waited.

I knew I would get better. In mid-January, still in bed, I created this image. It took me no more than ten minutes to cover the canvas.

The thinnest layer of paint reflects everything that had happened.

Then I got up and prepared lunch, my first meal in days.

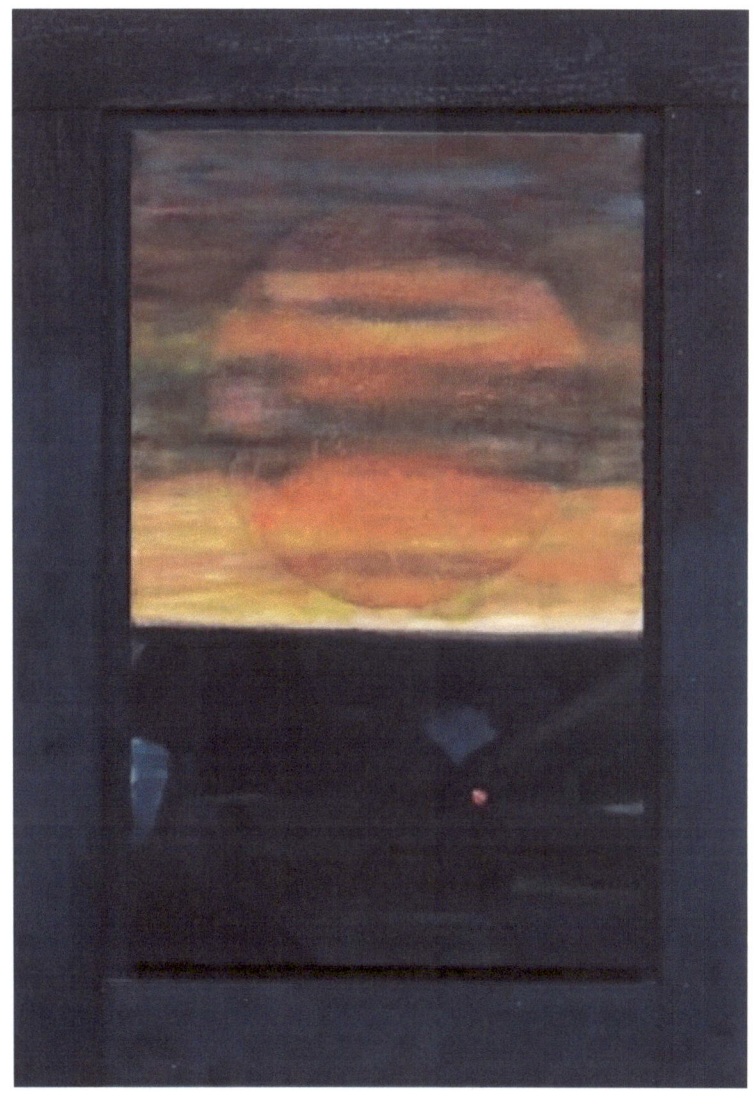

The Last Fire on Earth (2008)
Acrylic on canvas, 30"x20".

This painting is part of the 'Scorched Earth' series. It depicts a once fertile world that has lost the final battle for the planet's survival. One day, all biological life will cease to exist and much of it will have dried up and burned.

Fire is destructive. However, in some places, nature is adapting. This is particularly evident in Africa, where most of the world's fires occur, and where people use them to clear shrubs and trees in order to cultivate the land. I now know that this happens and has happened in many other places.

Rodica's Portrait (2007)
Acrylic on canvas 50cm x 50cm

The image below, titled 'The Lovers', is an oil painting on paper created in Kingsbury Road.

I should have read up on oil painting beforehand, but I didn't. Using paper as the medium for my first painting in London was a mistake, and it was also one of my first gifts to Rodica.

Rodica has an unlimited capacity to motivate people. She gave me a second chance at life. It was only when I was middle-aged that I finally understood the meaning of happiness simply by being around her. From the moment I took up painting and writing, she was always there to encourage me.

Painting her portrait was an act of devotion. It took me months to complete, and there were times when I was overwhelmed by doubt because I didn't know how to proceed. I changed the background several times before finally settling on a deep reddish brown. I wasn't able to paint her hair, so I decided to leave it short. Despite my many hesitations and the fact that I had to paint a face twice the size of normal and use a lot of layers to cover the skin, Rodica's portrait is special because it glows uniquely in low light.

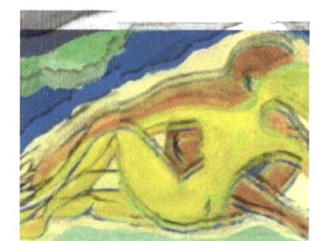

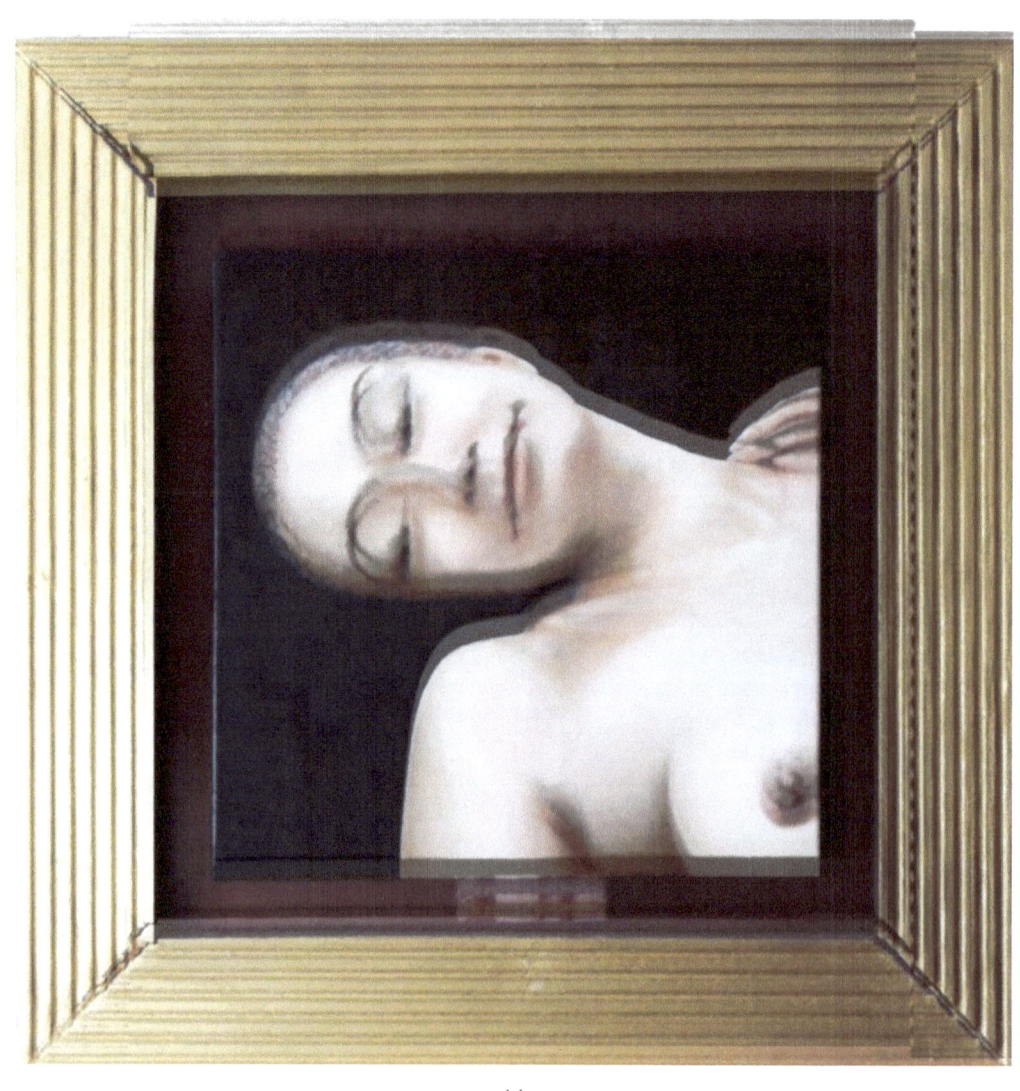

Calm Before the Storm: Earth, Water, Air and Fire (2008)
Acrylic on canvas 90cmx90cm.

This is the world as it was before its inevitable demise. Ancient European philosophers proposed that the world consists of four elements: Earth, Water, Air and Fire. If we go back two thousand four hundred years in history, what would the world be like today if Democritus' ideas had prevailed? He proposed that matter and everything else, including thoughts, were composed of atoms.

Had ancient statesmen accepted his ideas, science and technology would have progressed rapidly. Instead, we experienced a period of historical obscurity and dangerous ideas that still dominate parts of the world today.

This is why I painted Calm Before the Storm, which is also part of the Scorched Earth series. It depicts the planet's inevitable demise. Of course, before the storm comes, there will be a boom, which is probably what we are experiencing now.

Time will pass and fire will prevail when the Earth is absorbed by a red sun many times larger. Biological life will have been wiped out thousands of years earlier. Until then, why not cherish our Earth, the only one we have?

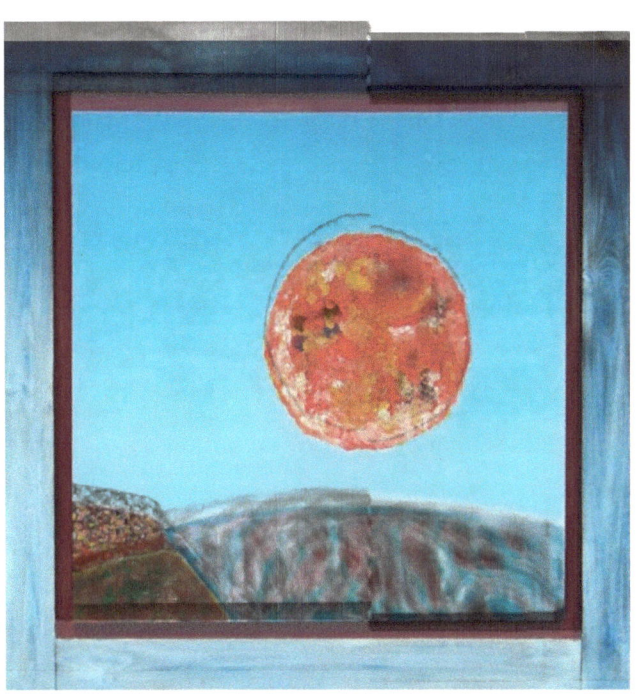

The Painting with no name (2008)

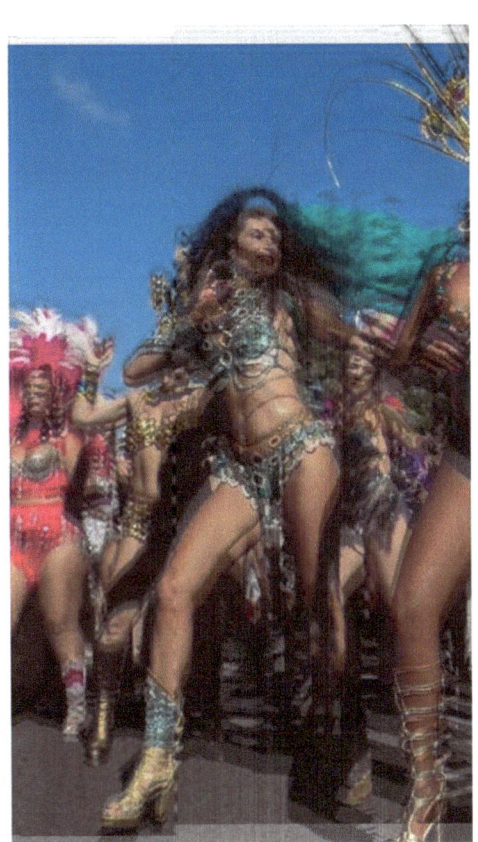

How could something so "horrendous" be someone's favourite work of art?

My neighbour was African, and perhaps the forms and colours in this painting evoked some type of nostalgia for her. When her son had grown up, she came to visit me to show him the colours of her favourite painting.

In this sense, beauty is in the eye of the beholder. Most of my ideas are a reaction to something I have read, seen, or heard. In the case of this painting, for instance, I was inspired by some sad news shared by someone very close to me.

Despite knowing that her daughter had a dangerous illness, requiring extreme discipline, medication and a proper diet, she was more concerned with maintaining her perfect figure. She wanted to be a size-zero model (she changed when visited Brazil). In fact, she had been a model before. I was shocked that she was endangering her life to be beautiful. I reacted by painting this picture quickly.

Expressing my feelings through the use of hellish colours enabled me to convey my disapproval of the absurdities of social life – in this case, when "being cool" means "being limited" and "dying to be pretty". I would rather remember her at her best, long after her zero period, dancing joyfully in the streets celebrating Rainbow Day.

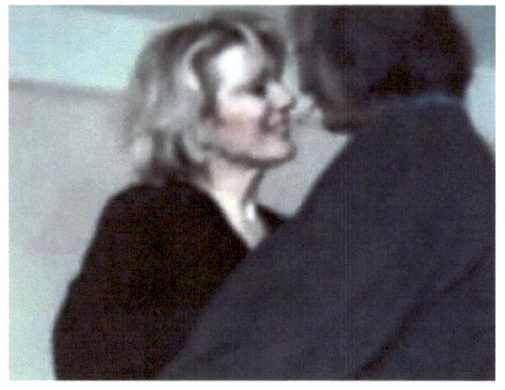

Hope and Freedom (2008)
Acrylic on canvas 90cmx90cm.

It is a portrait of Jutta Walmsley, who is German but British by marriage. It is a prime example of the exaltation of a muse. It is the only painting I have offered on canvas. It now belongs to her.

Passion exalts inspiration. Jutta's face was adjusted with minimal effort while the paint was still wet. The eyes, mouth, movements and shadows were painted quickly and without layers, making it difficult to reproduce or imitate. It took only one hour to paint her over a background that had been prepared in advance. The proportions of her body are light yet elongated. This reflects how she looked when I met her: a beautiful, middle-aged woman trying to escape a dead marriage and find a new lease of life. In short, she was looking for hope and a new future.

It was only after showing this portrait to her two children that Jutta became convinced of the blue face style.
They asked her,
"Mum, who painted it?"
The courage and passion she has for her new life are reflected in the many poems and short messages I wrote to her.

When she was young, she had a privileged life. This is not always beneficial, particularly with regard to future expectations. In our casual friendship, it seems that my role was to provide catharsis, helping her to reconcile her memories of her former life and the reality of being a free adult again after a long period of marriage. Her sister was also in a difficult personal situation. After the separation and divorce, Jutta became stronger, finding a new direction in life.

Jutta no longer needed me. She probably did not realise how much she had changed, and she cried on the day that I wrote a short poem about the moment when our friendship ceased to be nurtured by a connection of souls.

The poem begins with the line, 'My muse died this morning'.

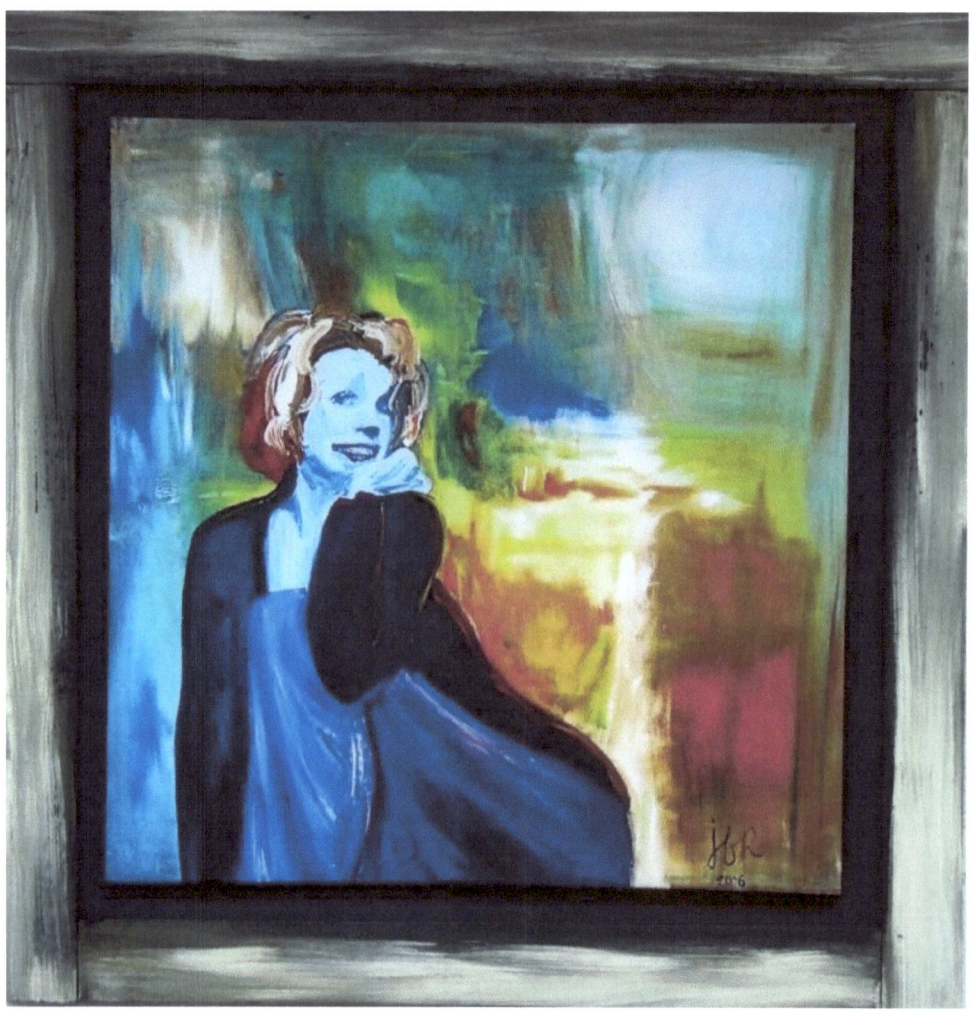

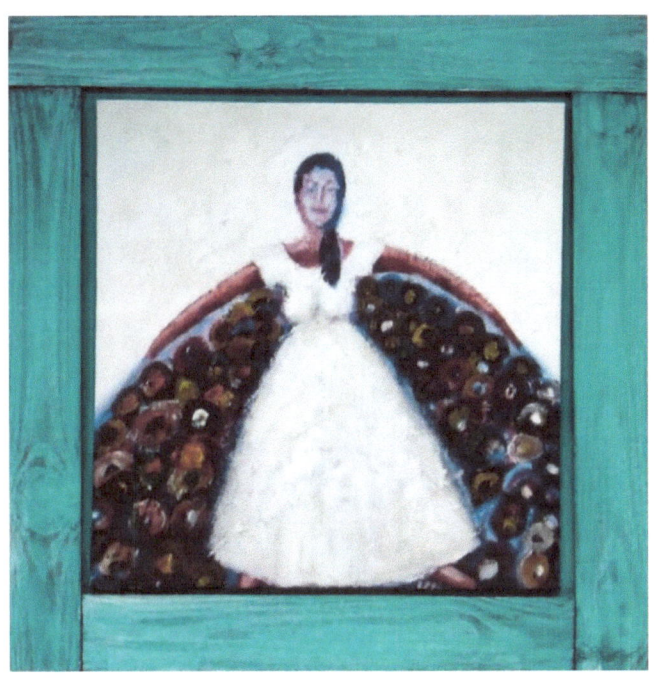

The Ovary (2008)
Acrylic on canvas 40cmx40cm.

Women are the guardians of their eggs.

Women are born with a complete, lifelong supply of eggs. Each ovary is a container of human life and the repository for the reproduction of our species.

No matter how old they are or where they go, girls and women carry this totality of potential life with them. As long as they live healthily and avoid accidents, this reality cannot be changed.

Girls are aware of this from a very early age and tend to mature faster than boys of the same age. This is the most important period of a girl's emotional and physical development. The time of the month serves as a reminder of the wonders of life, as well as pain, worry, and blood. They live close to the harsh realities of life and are naturally prepared to take care of their future children.

But what about boys or men? They have to learn everything in the abstract. Fathers-to-be will finally feel grounded when they see their first baby.

The Olympic Bronze Medal (2008)
Acrylic on canvas 80cmx60cm.

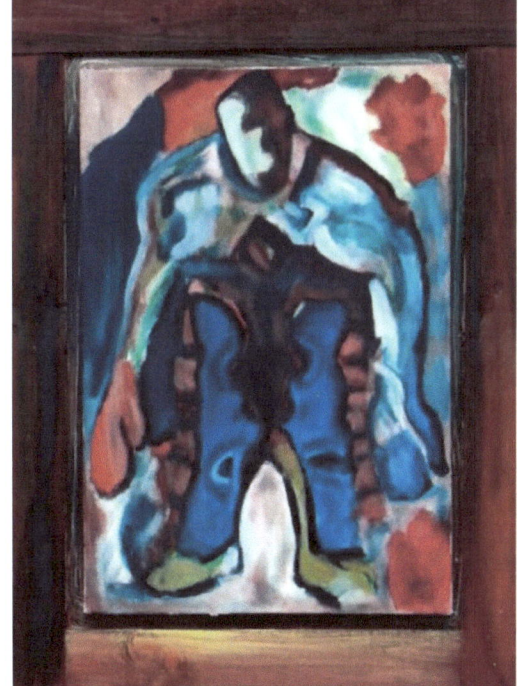

My initial idea was to publish my poems alongside illustrations. At the time, visual expression was more important to me than words, so it made sense. However, at the time of publication, including illustrations made the book too expensive, so I abandoned the idea.

The burst of creativity I experienced during this period was a liberating way of defining my new identity in London. This illustration is accompanied by a poem that is a strong cry about the entrenched and rigid principles that once defined my life. These principles were untenable in this Britain, where law and order still exist. The arrogant, self-confident man from Angola had softened.

The 2008 Olympics revealed a strange arrangement to me. In boxing, for example, two competitors always win the same bronze medal. In other words, they don't compete against each other for third place.

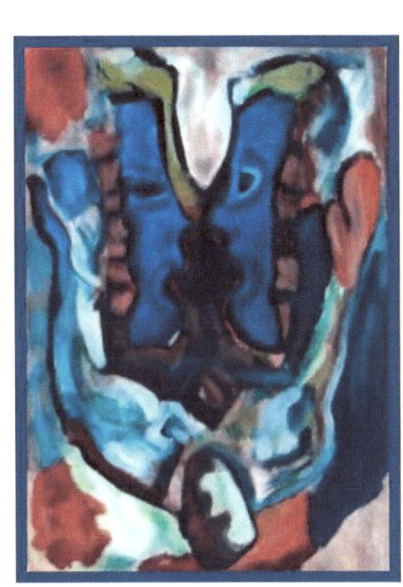

In a world of greed and competition, this fact was strange to me.

When I painted this work, I wanted the boxer to be sad, unhappy, gloomy, dissatisfied or incomplete because he did not finish his competition.

The reverse image on the left shows two faces obsessively saying to each other:

'I'm the best!'

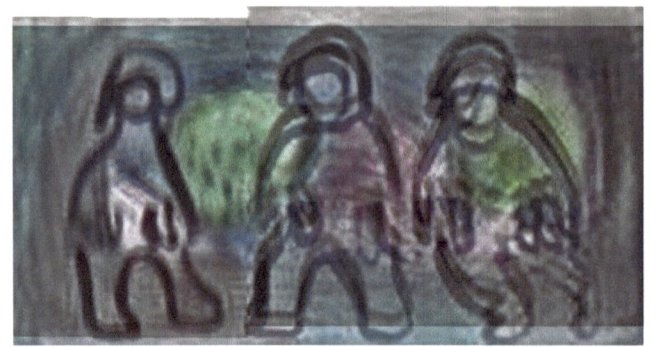

The Twelve Gordns, or The Twelve Apostrophes of the 2008-09 Credit Crunch Greedy Gang
Acrylic on canvas, 120cmx50cm.

In 2008-09, news about the credit crunch dominated the media. At the time, Gordon Brown was both Prime Minister and head of the commission that regulated the UK's banks.

Gordon let down the British people by failing to act against the banks and credit institutions, allowing them to imitate their US counterparts by lending money to private citizens and businesses without any sense or control. Hysteria prevailed in human behaviour.

The Twelve Gordns was inspired by the sketch "Three Ghosts" (pictured above), which depicts figures in a fog in front of an oncoming car. In the larger image, each of the Gordns has a name and has something to say about the present or the past.

On the right is my shortest poem. It is about people being reduced to nothing by the system, regardless of the ideas that govern it.

It is also about people's behaviour: those in power, and those who feel empowered even though they are not.

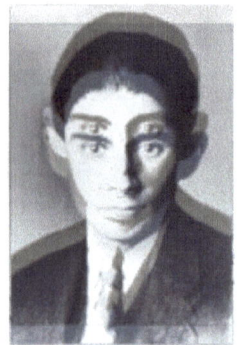

Epitaph
for
Franz Kafka

K. in life
K: in death

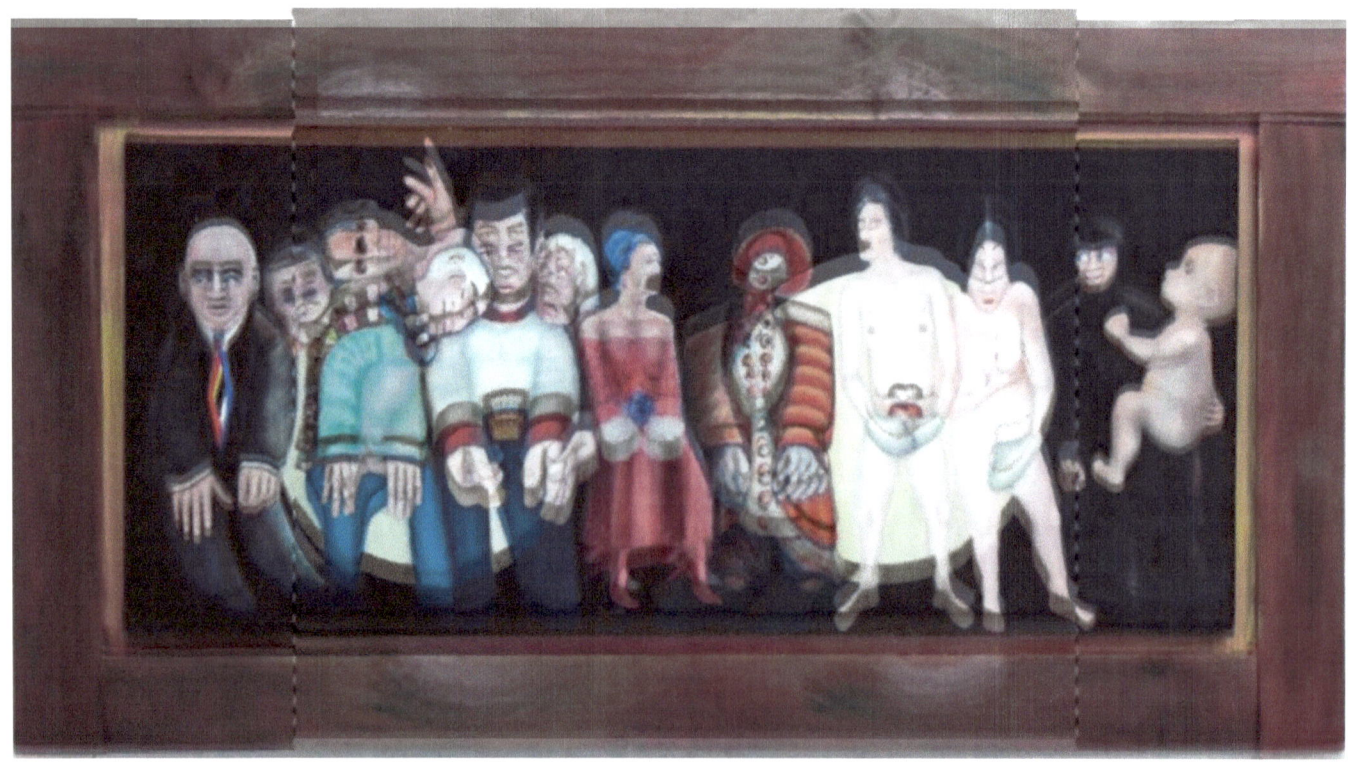

The Twelve Gord'ns Pamphlet

I was outraged when my bank offered me a loan knowing I could not repay it. Horrified, I created this pamphlet to distribute to the public.

My workplace, the Crown Prosecution Service, was a system that combined common sense with political correctness. However, a colleague and union representative told me that if I distributed the leaflet anywhere in London, I could be charged with a crime and sent to prison (he used the word 'racism').

Coming from Angola and having known so many different tribes, not to mention my own culturally mixed personal life, I found all of this very strange. Me, a racist? Was it all about the confident girl laughing at the corruption and decadence of the other characters? She is laughing at the oppressors and how greedy they are. In my simple view of the world, I saw her as an equal, not as my union colleague saw her. This will not be the first time that I have called people like my colleague 'Liberal-Guilty'; to me, they are a dangerous sort in the long run, or 'goody-goodies seeding bad deeds'.

Unfortunately, many people who believe in a religion or other ideology, or who are part of a group, clan or tribe, think they are superior to others. This is a common human trait, but it is also one of the main causes of racist behaviour, especially where different cultures and classes coexist. A stable, safe society can help diminish these innate behaviours.

I first encountered this British reality in London while learning English as a foreign language in 1994.

I noticed a pamphlet on a school noticeboard that had the word 'Kafir' written on it several times. I was confused. With an extra 'f', it would have been an offensive and racist word used in South Africa. Out of curiosity, I read the text. It was propaganda, and I immediately had a bad feeling about it. The word itself was different, but the text still seemed to glorify racism. The language the author used to express their ideas upset me. I felt accused, and my knees began to shake. I was transported back to the civil war in Angola, from which I had recently arrived. Each side of the conflict had its own absolute interpretation of the truth, which they believed justified the killing of those not in their faction. I had friends on all sides and many had been killed already.

Not many years later, murders began to occur in London and around the world, all in the name of religious purity. At the time I had to ignore the militant leaflet that demanded dangerous social polarisation because the school tolerated it. Such was the peace that was forced on us until it exploded. Nothing has changed, and many people continue to lie and conspire against innocent people to gain all types of social upper hand.

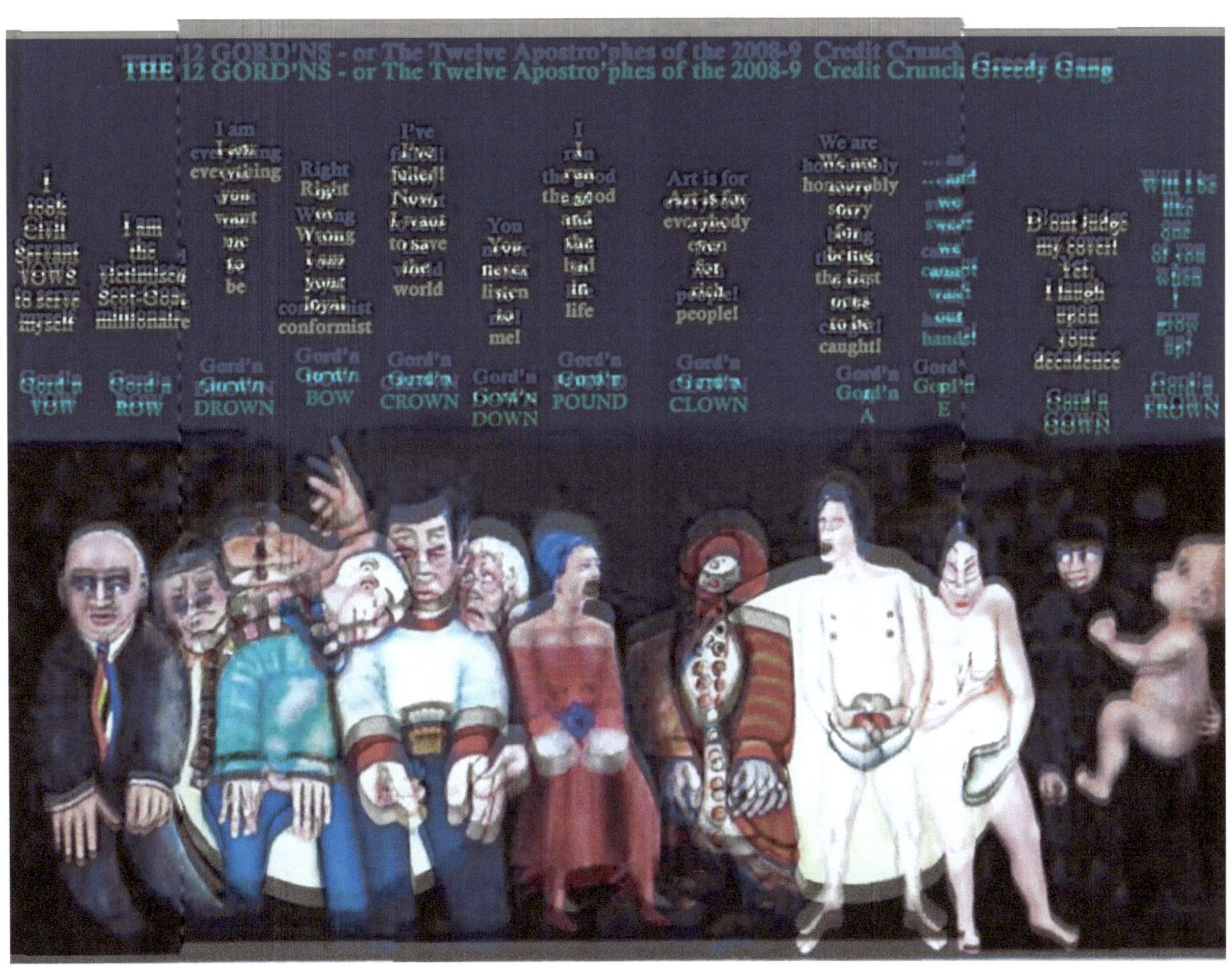

Madonna and Child (1975-2010)
Acrylic on canvas 90cm×90cm.

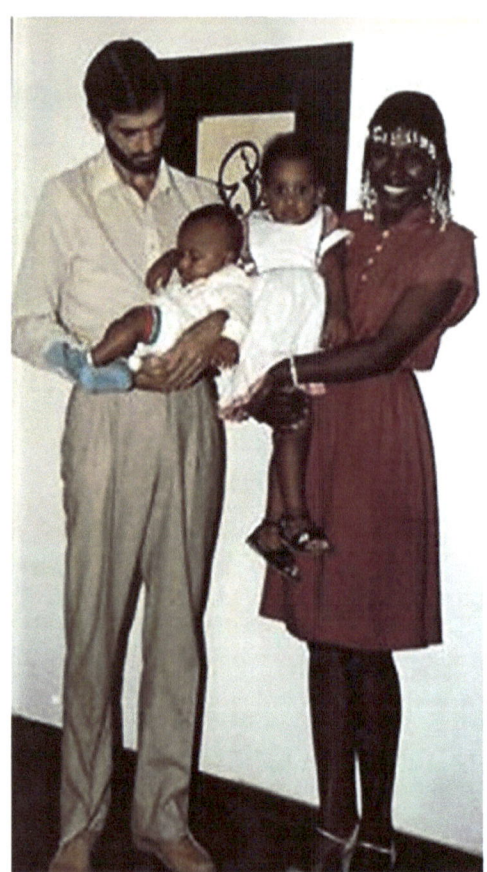

The bond between mother and child is so strong that they should have just one head.

In 1975, I painted two original versions of this image in acrylic on white A3 paper.

The one pictured behind our young family was lost when the glue on the back started to stain the image.

I gave the second original to a late friend, Josefa Medeiros (known as Pepita), and I do not know if that work still exists.

I was surprised by the strange reaction of many visitors (both men and women) to the work.

They saw a sexual act rather than a mother and child in unbreakable communion.

I was confused that they could not discern the aspirational side of the image, of the mother and baby being one.

I made a sculpture based on this painting. Unfortunately, the work was lost.

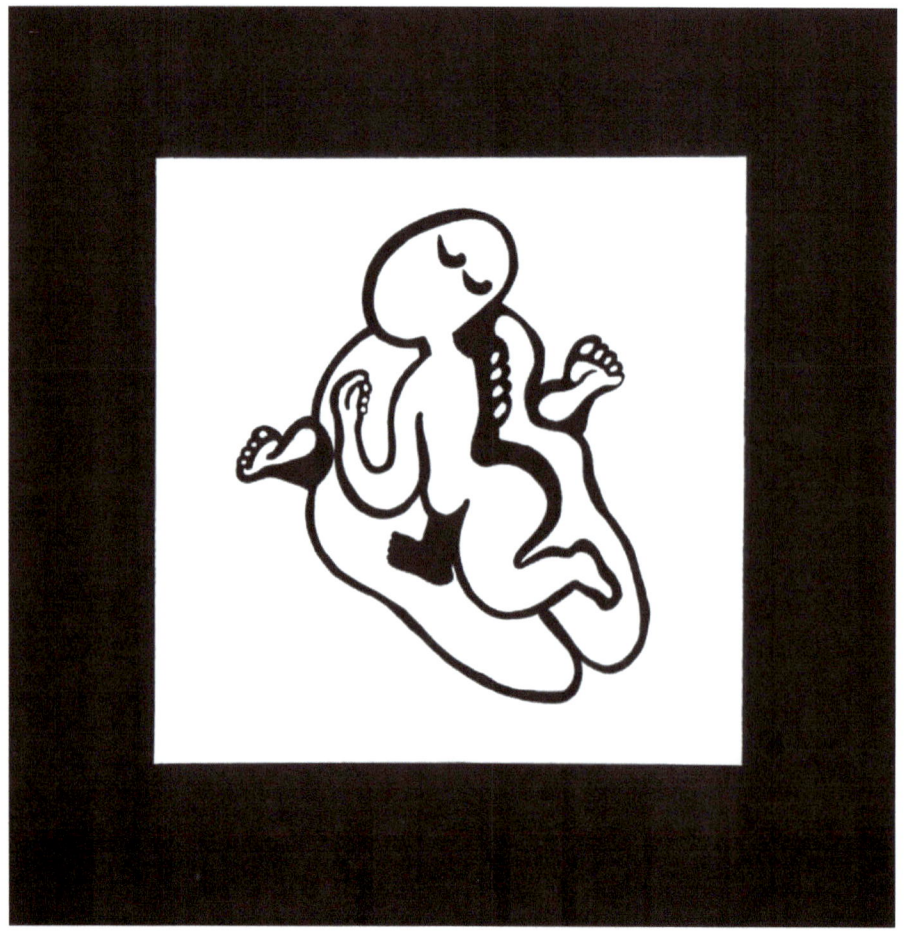

The First Wrinkle and Botox (2010)
Acrylic on two canvases, each 80cmx60 cm.

This piece comprises two side-by-side canvases: the painting on the left is a reproduction of an original sketch intended to illustrate one of my poems. The painting on the right is a depiction of a concept I developed after reading an article about wrinkles and Botox.

Human beauty is an odd concept. I believe it all started with people wanting women to be healthy and strong to ensure the survival of their group. It's all about small groups, not an abstract humanity. Then came progress, and with it, privilege. Power and competition forced people to do whatever it took to stay young and be the most beautiful.

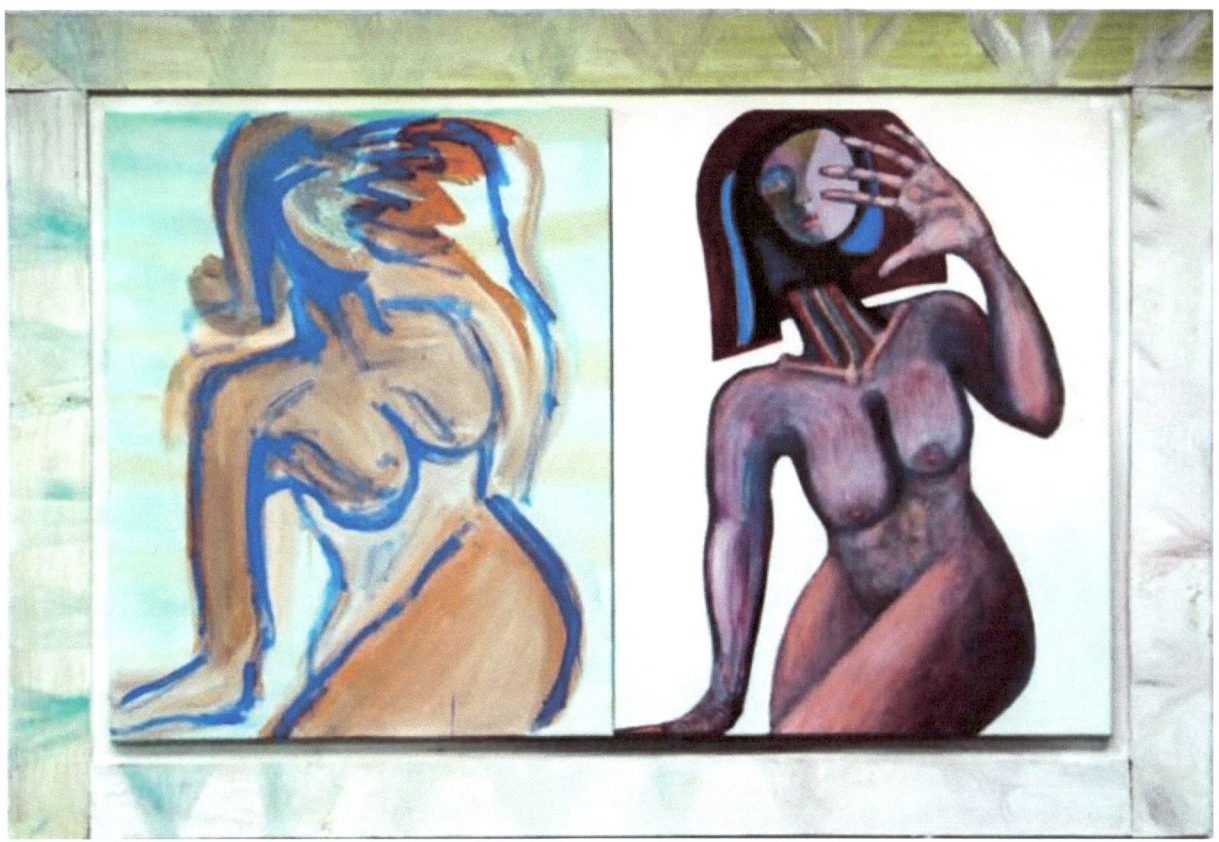

Historically, women in positions of power have been known to drink blood or semen in order to maintain their youth. Later on, some began to paint their faces. These foul treatments often damaged their bodies and faces.

I remember seeing a painting of Queen Elizabeth I in which her face was hidden by white paint: like a mask I think. This hid her real face from onlookers. Was it because her skin was damaged?

For many people, Botox is the current artificial solution to stop wrinkles forming. However, it also hides emotions by paralysing the nerves that control facial expressions.

Botox is a poison, and paralysed faces are no different to veils hiding them.

The image on the left shows the first wrinkle; the image on the right shows the flesh under the skin after Botox has been applied.

If a living body had no skin and was using Botox, would we be able to read its emotions from the raw flesh?

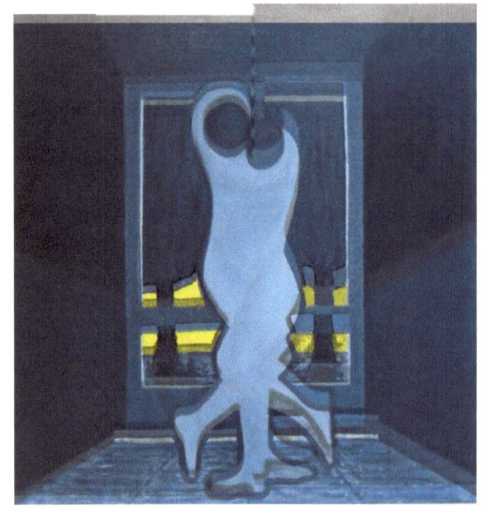

The Ghost of the Eight O'Clock Goodbye (2008)
Acrylic on canvas 90cmx90cm.

When I painted this memory in sombre colours, I knew nothing about Klimt. It was friends who made the association. One said the picture reminded them of The Kiss. Compared to the exquisite golden and colourful romantic paintings by Klimt, the quality of this work, a sad, dark canvas, is one in a billion, or zero to nothing. Yet my feelings are far richer than any artwork by a master.

This work is about longing. It was the eight o'clock nightly ritual: the time she had to return home, always at the same time, after I had made her feel beautiful and happy. This became unbearable.

Painting my emotional state was my way of acknowledging my feelings and reminding myself that I had no right to ask her for more.

I created these two loving figures during a boring class at National Salvador Correia High School in Luanda when I was 17 years old (in 1968). So, this is a memory that became a reality.

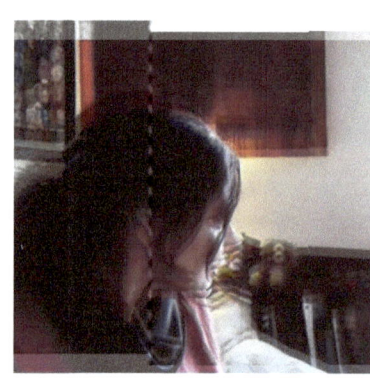

The Gates of Hell (2011) - Les Portes de L'Enfer Vivant
Acrylic on canvas, 90cmx90cm.

This work is an unfinished portrait of Astrida Berzina, a professional Latvian artist who is now approaching her eighties. I did not treat her very well.

She was an incredibly courageous person. After losing her status as a recognised artist in her country (the former USSR), she lost her job and all means of livelihood.

Her work was ignored in the West and never gained enough value to support her.

She came to London and worked hard until she retired.

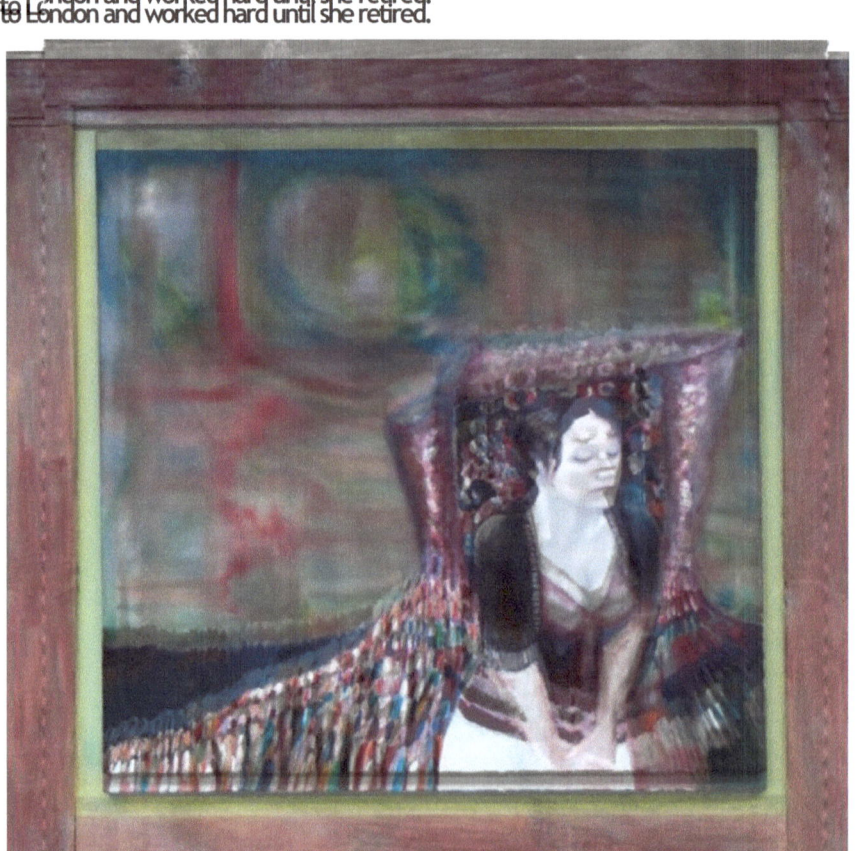

Homeless
Acrylic on canvas, 60cm x 80cm.

Sad and ill
I pay with my life
I still feel in my guts
The mould of my last meal

My life has been like a relentless rollercoaster ride. I have been homeless on more than one occasion, but I have always managed to return to a normal life. The poem that inspired this image was written in 1969, when I was living on the streets of Luanda in Angola.

Life on the streets is complicated. People end up there because they don't want anyone telling them what to do. We believe that no 'normal' person has the right to make decisions about our lives.

My father, a V.I.P., did not want me to be independent; he only cared about his reputation. He had absolute control over my life. One time, I became a submissive prisoner, confined to a room for seven months at a time, unable to experience freedom.

It was too much, and while he was away at an international conference, I got a job.

When my father returned, he forbade me from working. I complied. However, it didn't work out — his mistress, who was only six years older than me, didn't want me living with them. She lied and conspired, and my father was loyal to her. Against his image and reputation, I run away.

I was lucky. While waiting for the lights to go out so I could sleep in a V.I.P. box at the top of the grandstand far above the athletics tracks where he was cheering on a friend. He saw me before I saw him. It didn't take him long to guess what was going on. He took me home and his parents offered me free accommodation and meals for a few months.

My friend lent me money to buy the official, hallmarked documents. A prospective young civil servant needed these heavy, blue, stamped papers, which had to be filled in, acknowledged, notarised, and paid for. There could be no mistakes in any of them, and they had to remain valid for 45 days. Often, the first one had already lost its validity by the time the last one was finally obtained. All this paperwork was necessary to get a job.

Many young people who were still living with their families would get these jobs to save money so that they could get through the first few months of military service. That wasn't the case for me, though; it took me two years to pay back the loan to Jaime. Either way, homelessness was my reality.

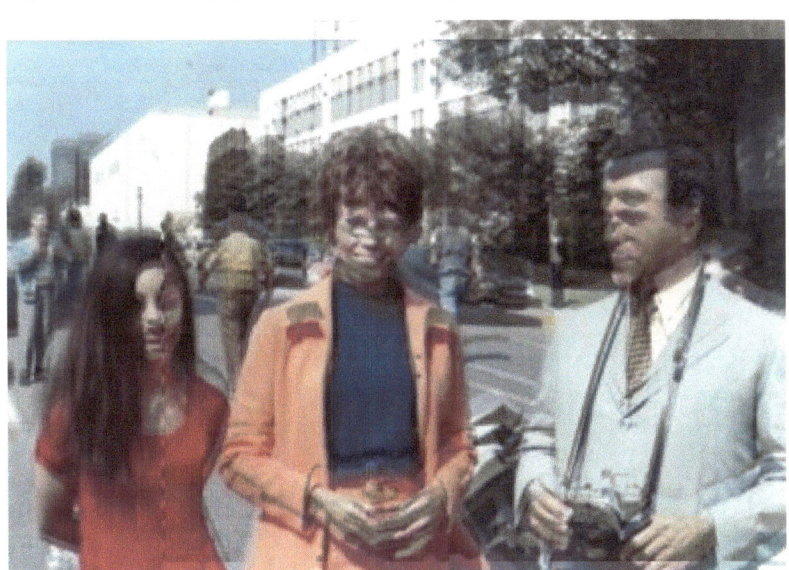

Photo taken in Salisbury, the former capital of Rhodesia (now Harare, Zimbabwe). On the left is Nelson Gaspar Pinto Fevereiro, who was then my father's mistress, or partner today. The woman in the centre is Paulina, an active social worker who was employed to assist local Luanda residents engaged in fishing.

Dream of Lightness
Acrylic on canvas, 80cm x 60cm, London, March 2011.

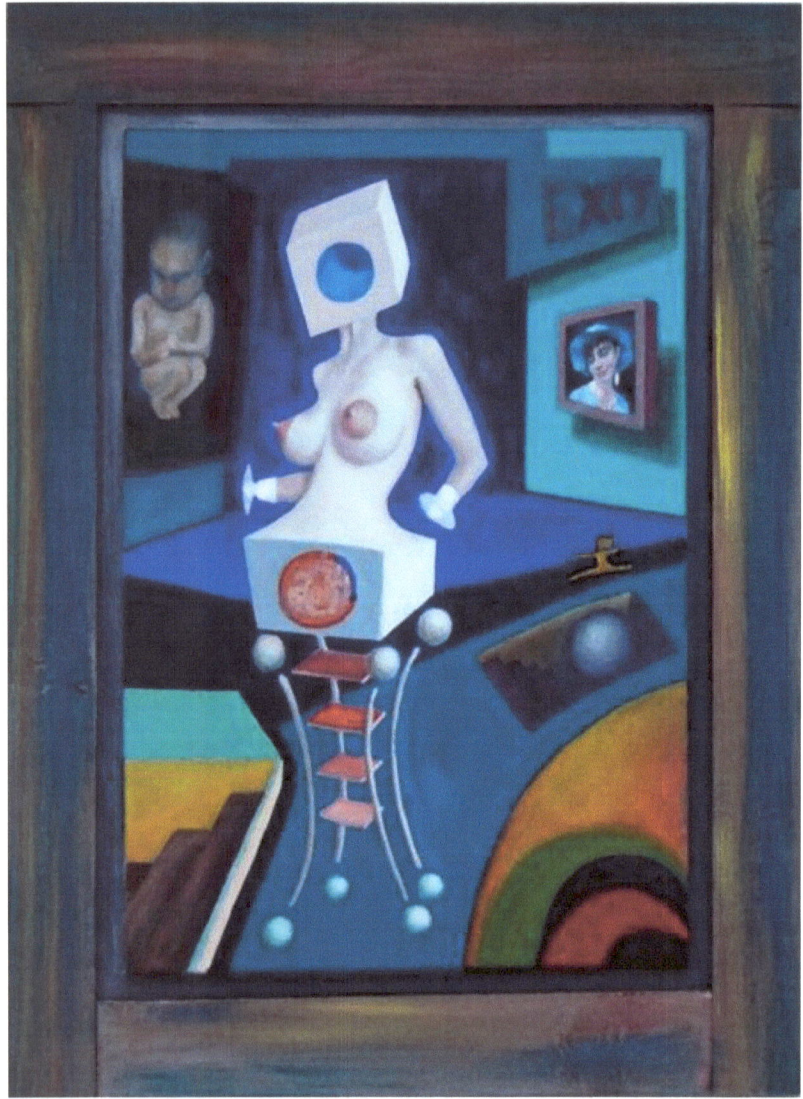

Every pregnancy is different. For some, it is a time of love and hope. It is often a time of transition between denial and acceptance, between seeing the situation in a negative light and embracing life.

It also is 'La Vie en Rose'.

Difficult pregnancies are a reminder that human reality can be crude and frightening. All mothers-to-be share the anxiety of wondering if their baby will be perfect.

We also know that mothers check their babies for perfect lips and that special smile after breastfeeding, which reinforces the bond between mother and baby.

Mothers also check their babies' fingers and toes.

It's the fear of the unknown.

As pregnancy progresses, expectant mothers become heavier, and the world around them seems full of obstacles and dangers at any given moment.

Gayton Road

*

The Muse
Acrylic on canvas 60cm x 80cm

How overwhelming can a muse be?
Is she a dream, a nightmare, a fantasy, or is she hope, future, or the whole world?
My experience tells me that she can be all that and more.
The image was a message to myself.

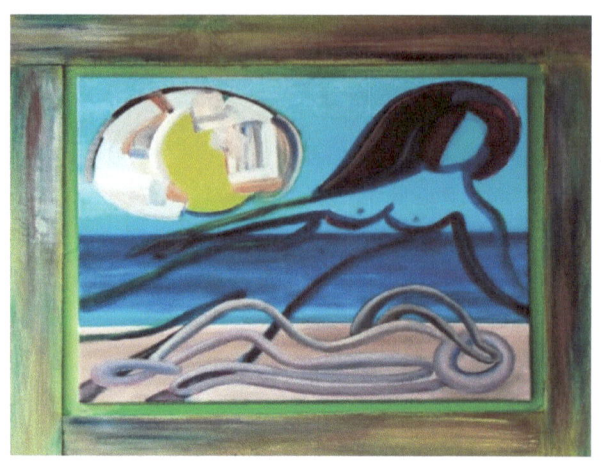

The Four Civil Servants Values (February 2011)
Honesty, Integrity, Impartiality and Objectivity, in colour and Braille.
Acrylic on canvas 90cmx90cm.

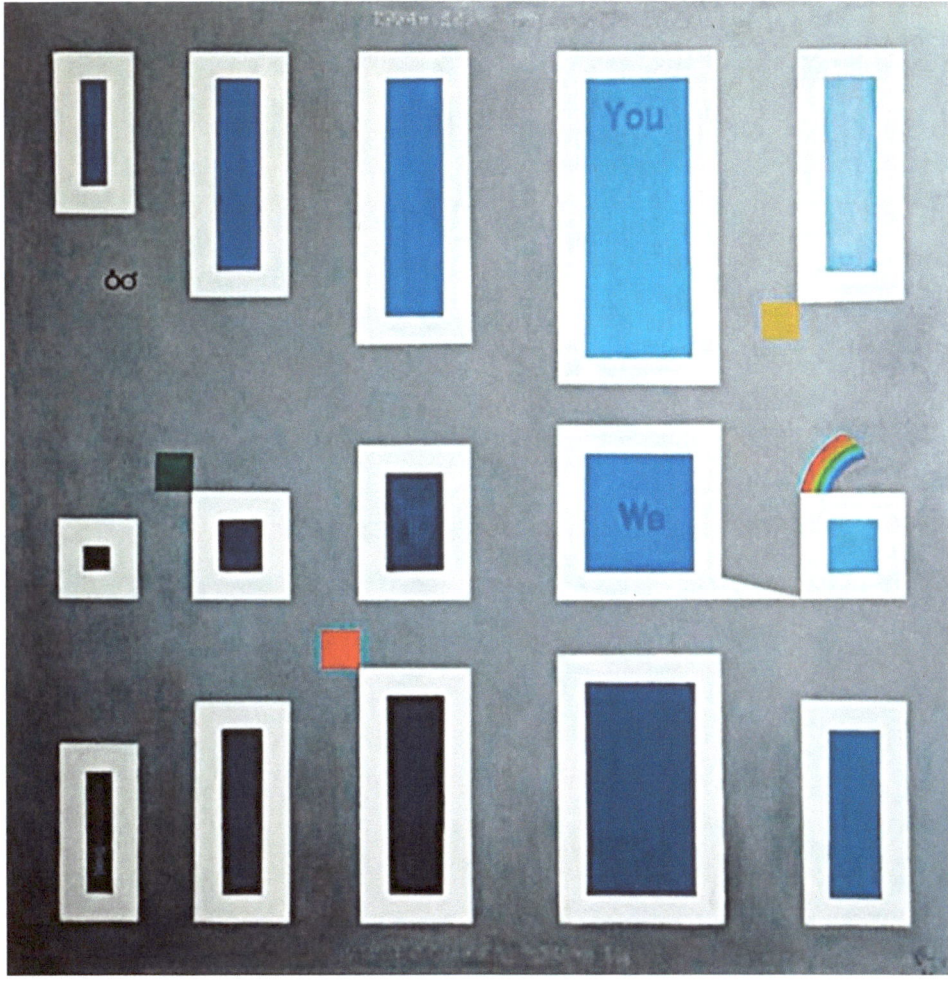

How can an art contest be turned into a tasteless event?

The answer is simple: get the judges to ignore the rules.
The organisation set the theme of the four values of the public servant. I followed them, strictly. The others?

The three finalists were a sculpture called 'Honesty', which was not intentionally created for the exhibition; a piece called 'RED', consisting of two spilled spots of red paint randomly thrown onto a white canvas; and this piece.

I used the pronouns 'I', 'WE' and 'YOU' to remind public servants who they work for. I serve/we serve YOU. Also, the blocks with pronouns vary in size, with the larger ones conveying greater responsibility. Two other features – colour and position – were added to highlight the importance of the subject. There is also a token reference to minorities, and the title is written in Braille.

The three judges were: Sir Gus O'Donnell (then the UK's highest-ranking civil servant), a former model who had posed for a famous painter, and a minor celebrity. They did not follow the competition rules, but at least they helped me to see sense in my indignation. Several people reminded me that ignorance and conceit are mundane realities.

Having arrived late to the event, the trio became the exhibition themselves by nonchalantly flaunting themselves around the exhibition. They won, sorry, they were the first prize.

The Former Cornerways Hotel
Acrylic on canvas, 60cmx80cm.

The photo shows a lodge where I rented a tiny flat. My medicinal DIY work is visible in the front garden.

The building has twenty-three rooms, most of which do not comply with UK housing regulations.

The old hotel was in need of renovation, but the local authority decided not to act, and the property continues to generate substantial annual income for the landlord.

I built a 12x5metre pavilion garage at the back of the building, but the local authority ordered me to demolish it. I complied but the rebel art exhibition lasted one week.

The painting depicts all the building's facades.

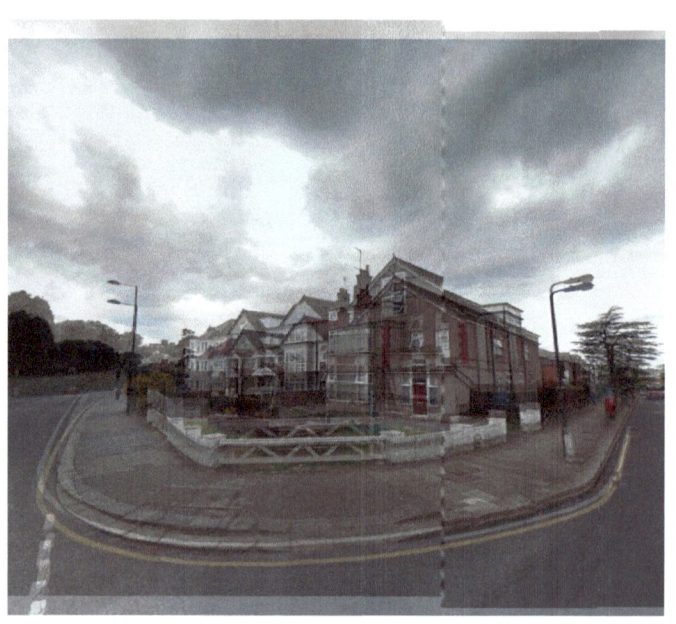

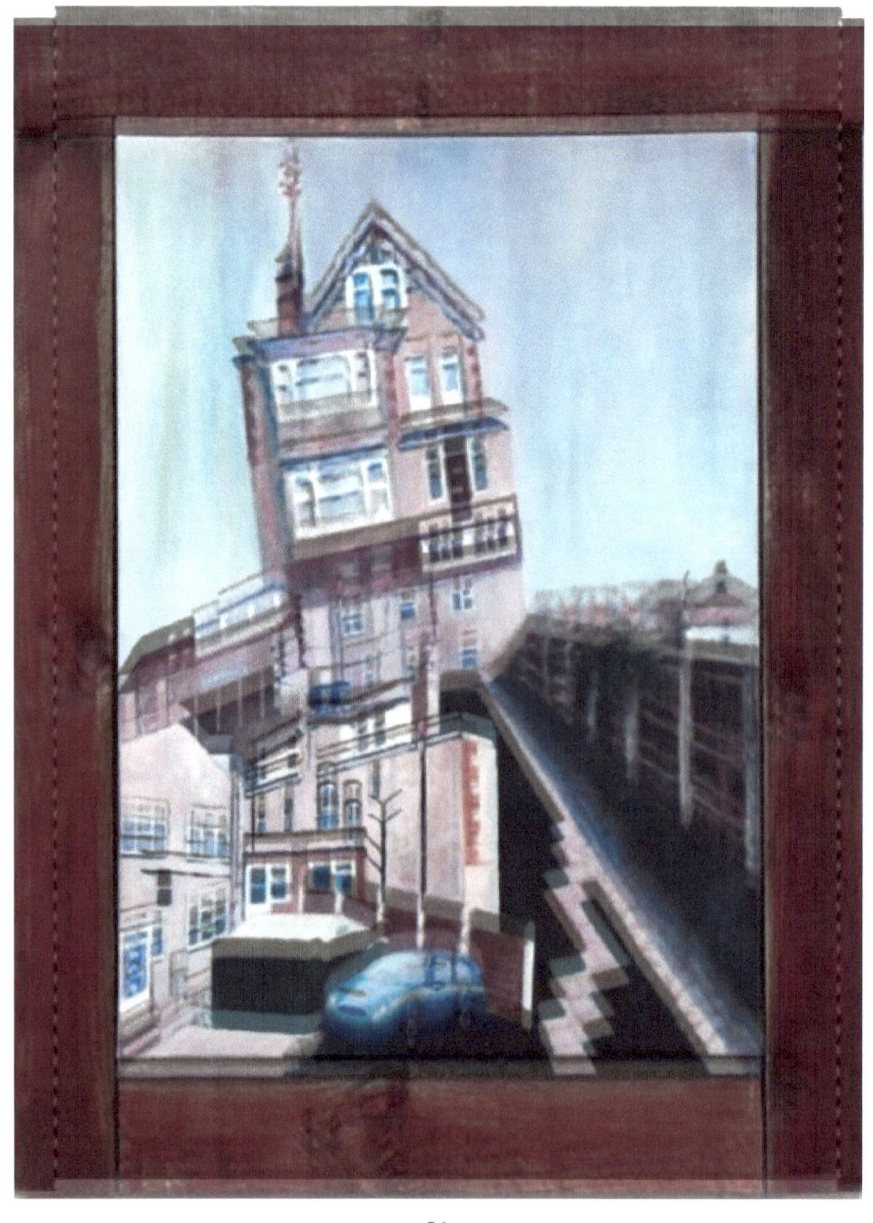

History of Portugal on the flag
Acrylic on canvas, 60x80cm.

John was born in Lisbon. After spending two years at the Military Cadets High School, the boy left the country to join his family in Africa. He was eleven years old. This child should have been a normal boy who should have loved the country of his birth, but instead he learned to hate it from the age of five.

In 1973, the first peaceful post-war year in Angola, he had lunch with a naval chaplain, the couple he was staying with, and the local governor of the Moxico province, who was also second in command of the Eastern Military Region. During the conversation about the recent events in the town, the two-star general unexpectedly announced the death penalty for the conscript sergeant who had allegedly committed a crime against Mrs Bonito-Perfeito, the wife of the commander of the local military regiment. A few days later, John was arrested by the political police and charged with the crime, so he knew he was facing the death penalty as it had been announced in his presence.

In the 'small-country', as people used to call the colonial country, the death penalty had been legally abolished in 1864. John was proud of this fact, because it was the first country in the world that did it. Not anymore, he then believed that he would be killed by the back door (sent on a military operation from which he would not return). This didn't happen, he got an alibi, but John kept on going not trusting anyone in a position of authority (since he was 5), let alone anyone from the 'small-country'.

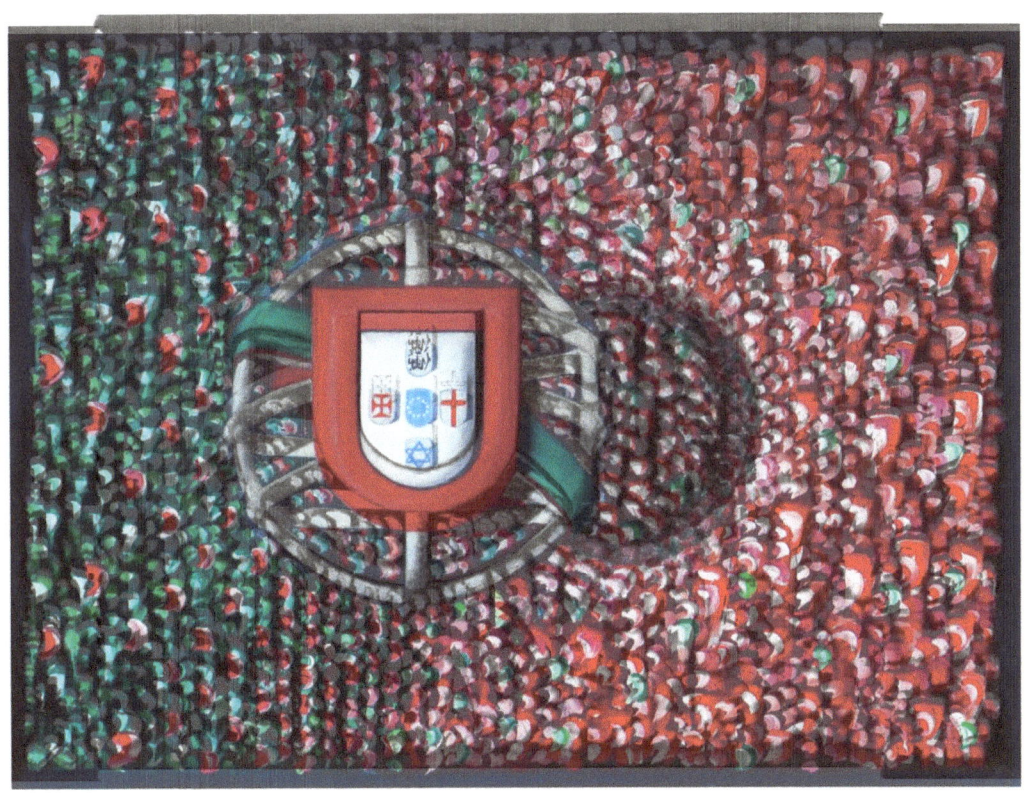

When I painted this flag, the world was in the grip of violent extremism. Religious acolytes were taking the words written in their scriptures a thousand five hundred years ago literally, in order to create the long-awaited and promised paradise on earth. About a thousand years ago, the country of my birth was occupied by the Moors. I depicted this using a crescent-shaped shadow trampling on people (a mixture of red and green comas). The shield contains five symbols representing historical events. Clockwise from the top: First, Norman princes who conquered the country from the Muslims; second, the cross of the Knights Templar, who helped the Christian population secure the coast and establish safe harbours for Crusader ships. This created a new European country. The next symbol is the Star of David, which reminds us of the plight of the New Christians (they faced religious persecution or assimilation into the country as Christians). The second cross represents the country's geographical discoveries and maritime trade around the world, as well as the colonial empire that emerged centuries later. Finally, in the centre is the small country as part of the European Union. After a long period under a fascist regime during which 85% of people were illiterate and unable to read even a short news article in a newspaper, it is reassuring to know that the new democratic laws are being respected.

Thomas Hewlett House

*

Waterspout on a Beautiful Day (2015)
Acrylic on canvas, 40cmx40cm.

While fishing from a small boat near the tip of the Island of Luanda, the capital of Angola, my brother Luis and I saw two whirlpools in the water. We were surprised to witness this phenomenon. It was a perfect day: the sky was blue, there was no wind, and the morning sun was bearable. Despite there were hardly any wind, the water rose in two parallel columns close together.
Making the moment even more special, the two thin waterspouts were transparent and never moved. On such a nice, windless day, there was no obvious explanation for what was happening.
The weather in Luanda is usually stable, with very hot and humid conditions. There is usually no wind in the morning, a soothing breeze at the end of the afternoon, and then no wind again in the early hours. With the exception of the equinoxes, there are no waves in the morning and the ocean is as calm as a pond.
Fifty years later, now living in London, I saw the news showing the immense misery caused by extreme weather in many countries. The columns of water I saw on TV were destructive, powerful tornadoes forming in dark, stormy clouds over the water.
Moved by the contrast between my own experience and these images, I imagined a powerful, rumbling tornado swirling in the sky above the paradise I had known, where I had once seen two small whirlpools. This may seem contradictory, but it reminds us that there is no such thing as a perfect paradise — nature is what it is, and we are part of it.

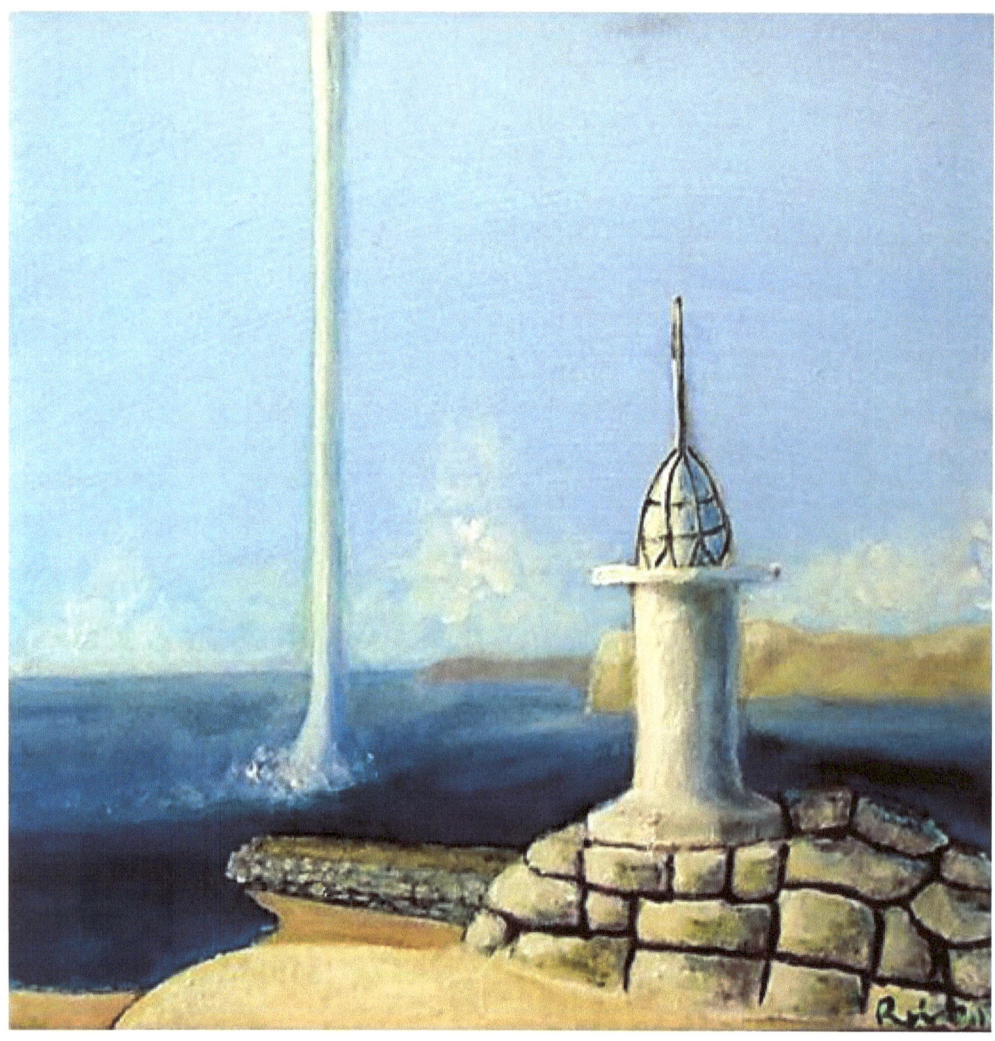

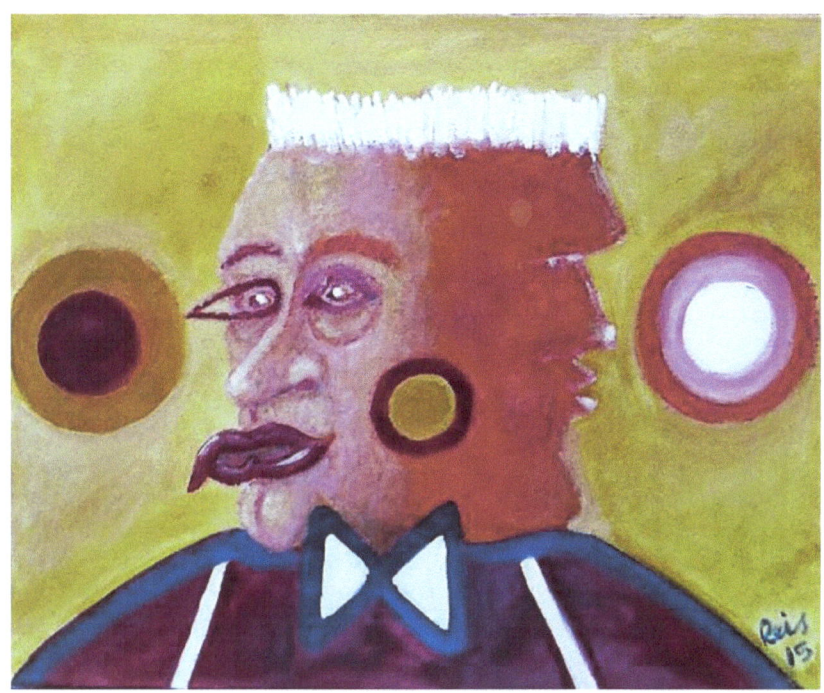

Two Faces (2015)
Acrylic on canvas, 40x50cm.

Memories of another person.

People like the way I was, a special person, are not capable of lying. After a lifetime of being antisocial, I finally learned to tell a few white lies. I now realise that people who can't lie are constantly at odds with others, especially when they lack common sense. I did not know the difference between all forms of lying, subterfuges, accommodating, and conforming. It was strange when people — managers and workers alike — would tell me, 'Phillip, watch out; protect yourself'. It was like asking me to walk without legs. Something was wrong; in consequence, trouble followed me everywhere.

With such shortcomings in my behaviour, knowing the facts helped me to cope. Facts were absolute truths that I could fight for and defend, even if it caused pain to others. But it was all in vain; I became even more absent-minded, seeking refuge in isolation.

As I couldn't make them fit me, I became frustrated and indignant. From there, it was a small step to living in permanent anger. All because people were always lying. It was disheartening; the world was full of hypocrisy.

When I came to the UK, I watched TV programmes to learn English. The English I had learnt at school was not enough. However, I lacked contact with people, and my isolation was not productive. The frustration made me worse.

Soon, I started watching TV debates on social issues. It seemed to me that the audience members were speaking freely and conveying open and honest messages with confidence.

I began to doubt myself: 'How can hypocrites, people, speak so reasonably?'

Gradually, I began to accept people for who they were — perhaps the first step in adapting to the country. The second step was more difficult; I knew I had to break down my internal barriers and learn to tell white lies.

It is never too late to learn, and finally, in my old age, I adopted a few of them: 'It's alright, you're alright, well done, all is well, have a nice day' (no one has nice days), and so on.

I still can't say the bigger ones, but I use 'right' a lot.

Anyway, I finally have two faces, so I'm almost normal!

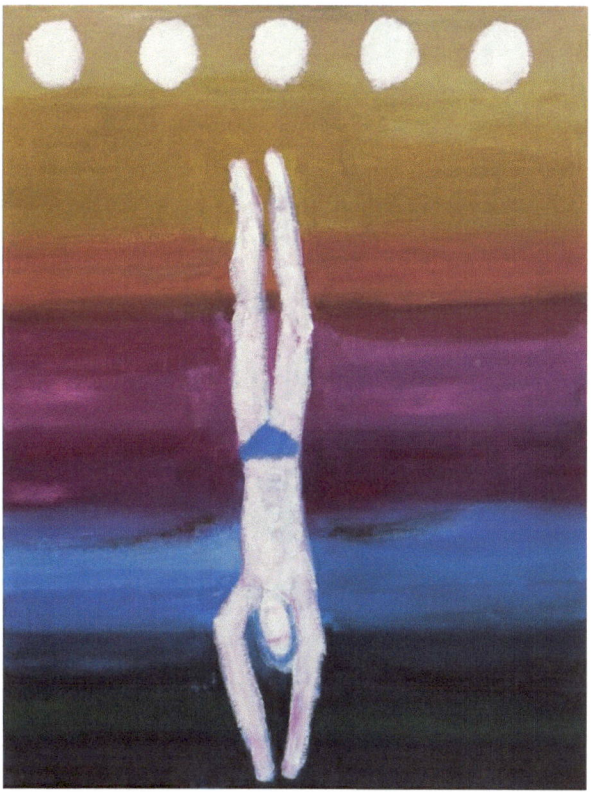

Diving into the Olympics (2016)
Acrylic on canvas, 40cmx40cm.

The dark green water in the Olympic pools in Rio de Janeiro, Brazil, triggered my interest. The water had become infested with algae, which proliferated explosively within a few days. The swimmers and divers had to use water that resembled a cauldron of decomposing vegetables more than the waters of a public pool in the highest international competition (a slight exaggeration). The association with diving in the dark was too strong to ignore, so I painted this study in a matter of minutes. The dark green waters were telling me something: "Stay still, don't dive into the darkness". It was another minute work.

Columbo's Migrants Flying Machine (2018)
Acrylic on canvas, 90cm×90cm.

This painting depicts Donald Trump's 'sonorous firecrackers', aimed at foreigners who did not look like him. It's about immigration. Having lived in an African country for nineteen years after its independence and twelve years before that, I cannot forget the decolonisation process. I witnessed deaths, massacres, destruction and negative foreign political alliances. But I also remember the influx of foreigners, including people from communist countries, such as Cuba, Germany, Bulgaria, Russia, Armenia, Azerbaijan, North Korea and Vietnam. Some of these people were my neighbours, as well as representatives from international charities and other organisations. There were also Western consular and embassy representatives, as well as their employees, who, unlike the 'internationalists,' or those from communist countries, enjoyed freedom of movement, something we all expected from anyone. Later on, we started seeing foreigner Africans looking for business opportunities, mainly from Senegal and Nigeria, as well as people from other parts of the world, such as Lebanon and Brazil. It was a new world with new religions and new crimes. The big world was invading the small one.

Despite the thousands of casualties (many of which were caused by famine) and widespread destruction, I also observed positive changes in the country in the years immediately following independence. People had known during the colonial era had grown in confidence and become themselves. A former carpenter, who was now a militant in the ruling party, was no longer angry. He was happy to see me – and I was the son of his former boss. All of this was happening around me. It was a revelation, even if it was sometimes difficult to accept, because some behaviours that had been forgotten or forbidden during the colonial era had returned, witchcraft believes for ex., and these were not always liberating.

The good thing mattered. I particularly remember a young girl who had once worked for Nelma, my father's mistress. After independence, she saw me at the roundabout called Maianga, an important landmark in my life in that capital. She was the one who stopped me. At first, I didn't recognise her – she was beautiful, exuding joy and confidence. She told me about her new life, then paused. Looking more serious, she said, 'You were right. Now I understand what you meant when you told me that Nelma was no good. I wasn't free. She was nice, but her niceness held me back.'

Seeing this girl glowing with confidence made me happy. It's hard to be right, but being able to be your real self is what paradise is all about. That is the meaning of liberation, not many saw this.

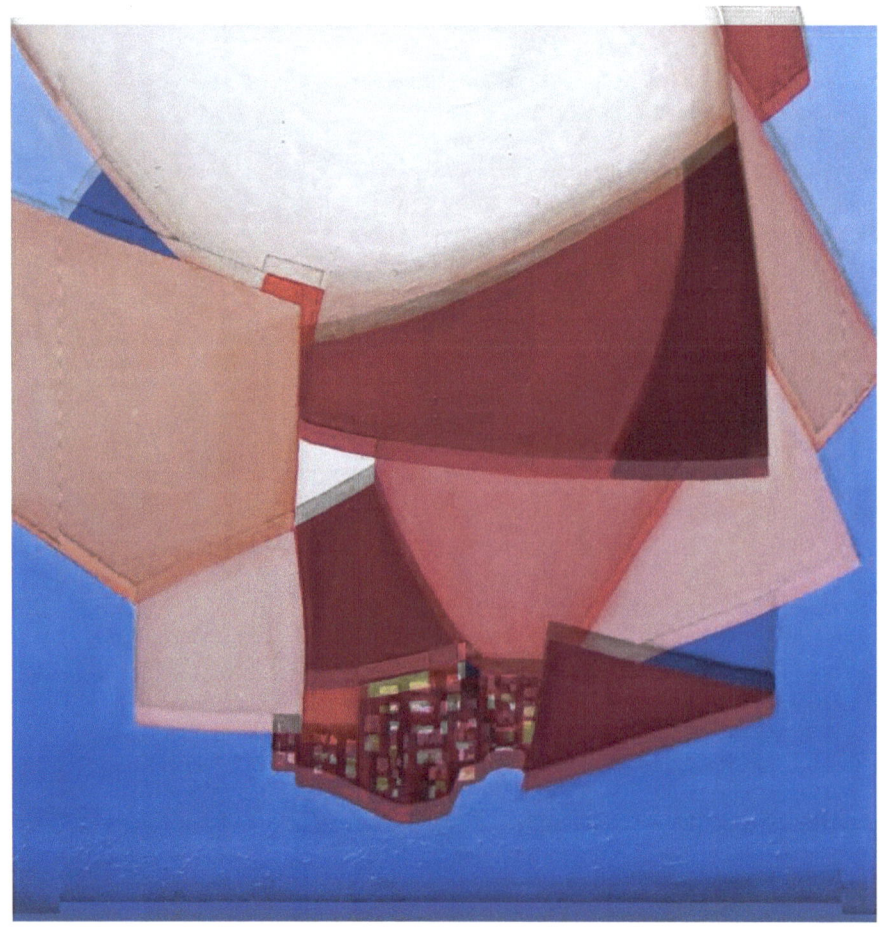

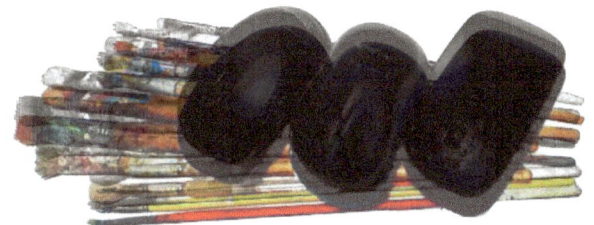

Pinner Road

Illustrations made for my poems - The Transition

*

Each poem in the booklet I AM WOMAN I AM has a related illustration; each one created in a whim. They were done in acrylic on ordinary A4 paper or A4 cardboard. To allow the paint to dry quickly, some illustrations were placed in the oven and this created in places textures in relief. Some of the illustrations were later used in paintings on canvas.

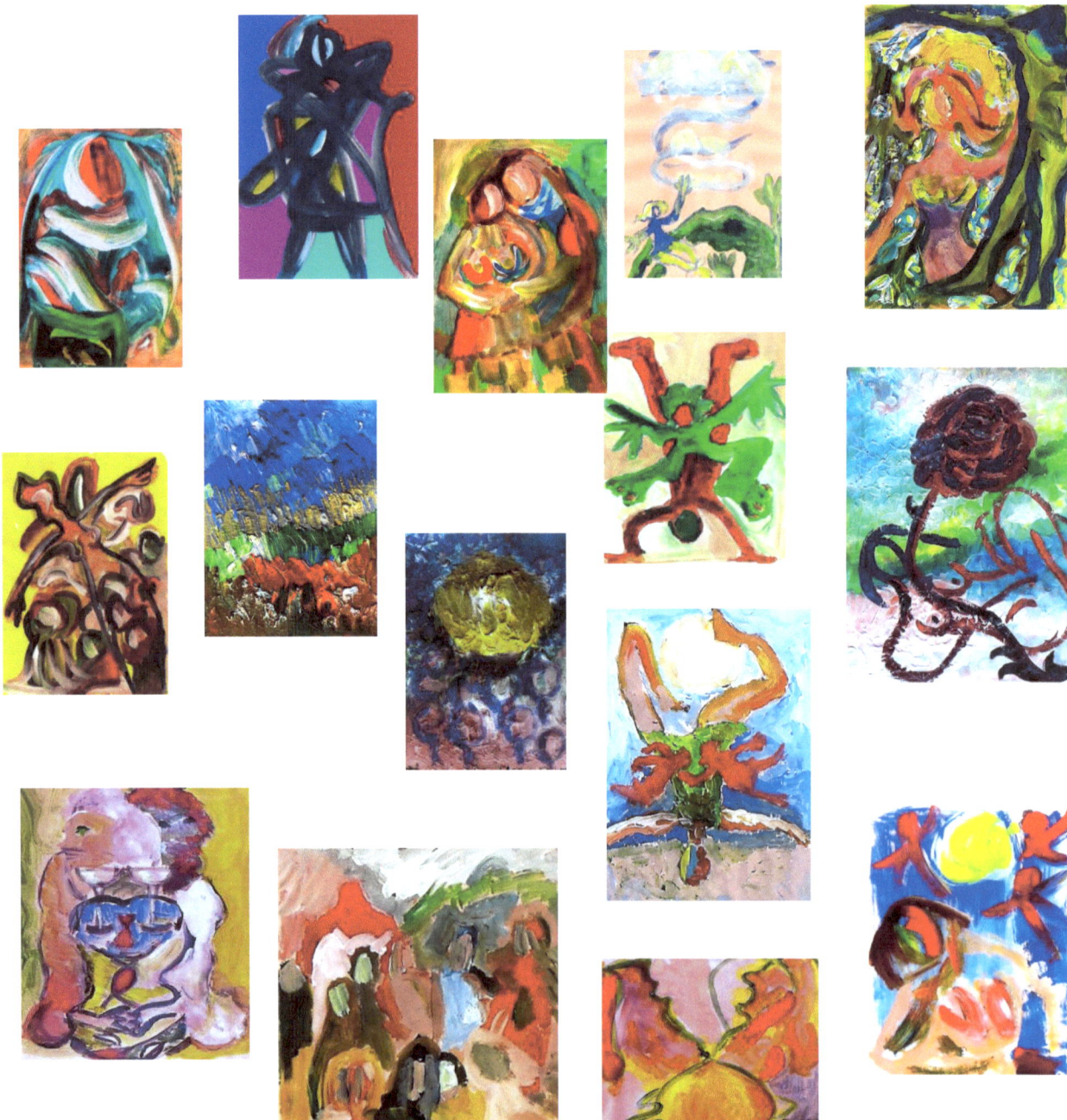

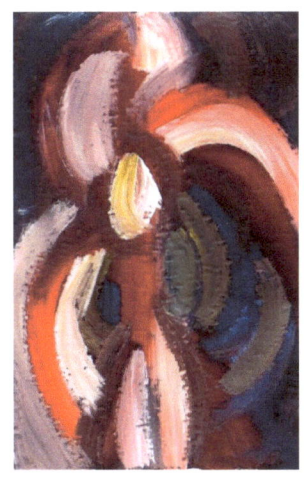
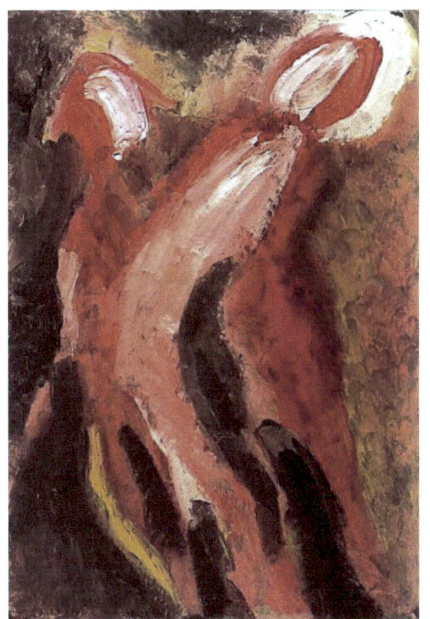
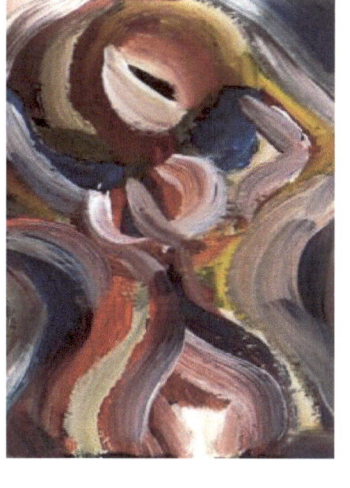
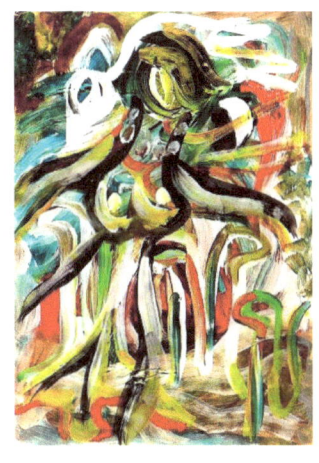
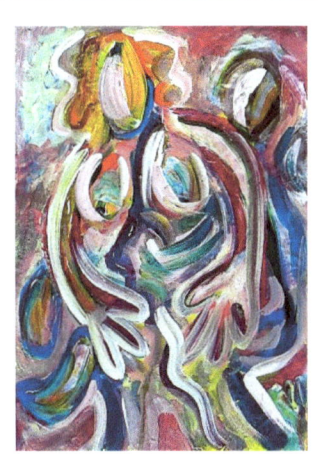
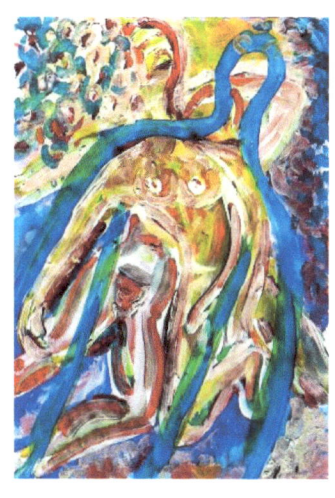
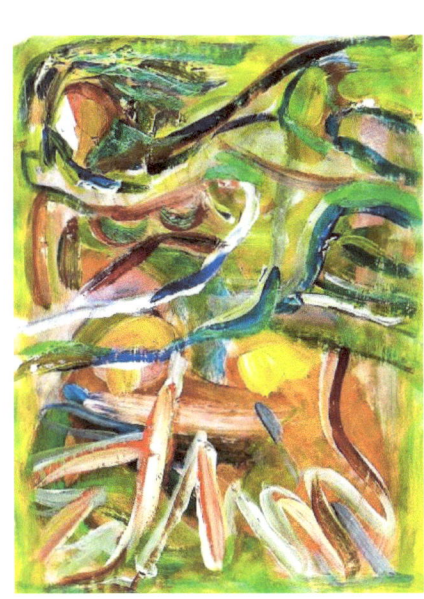
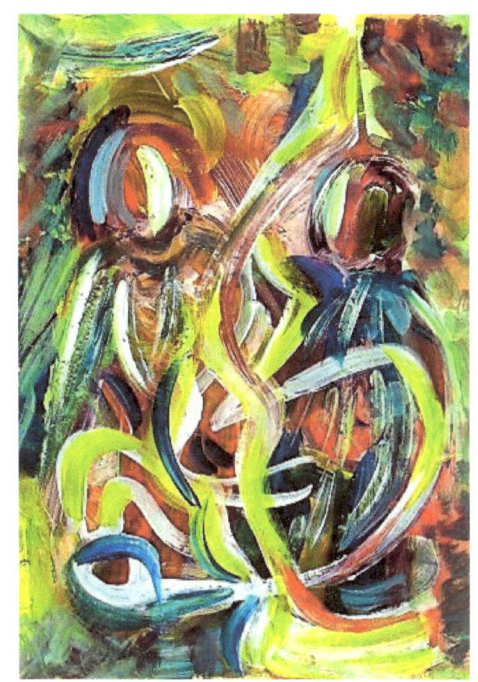

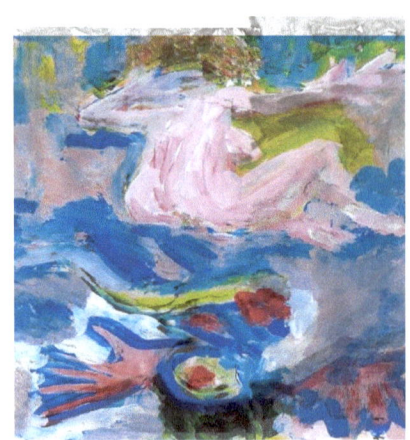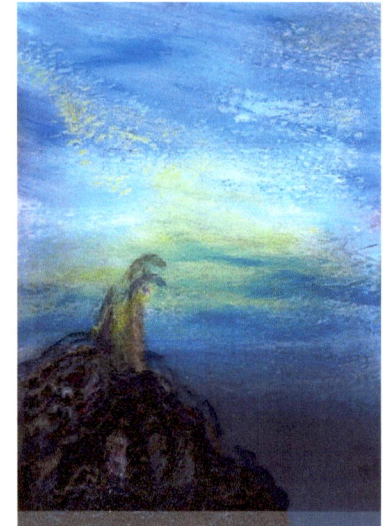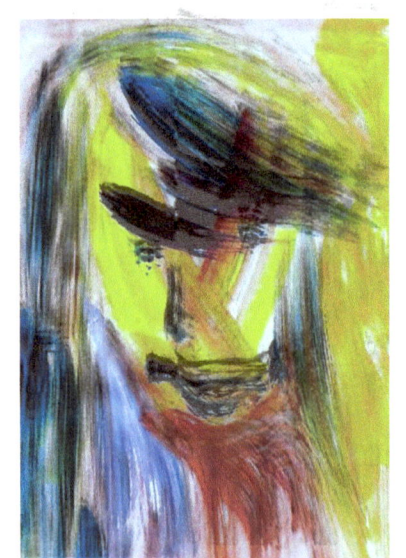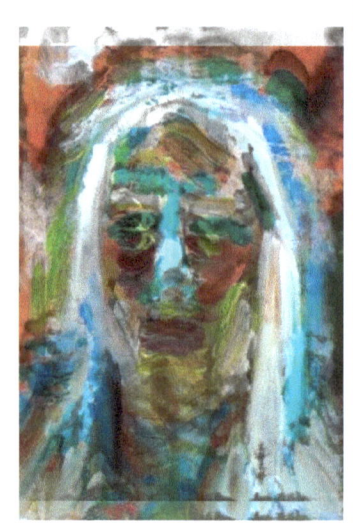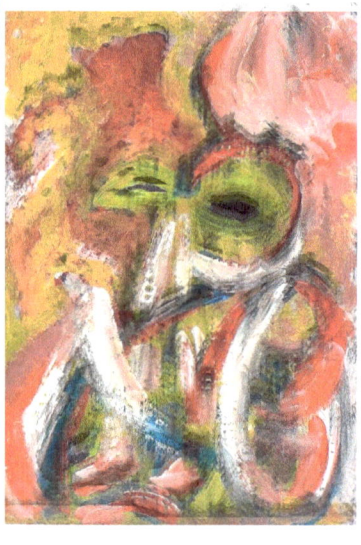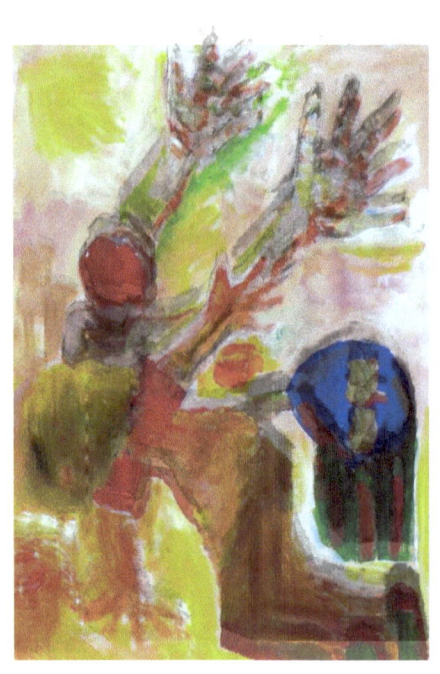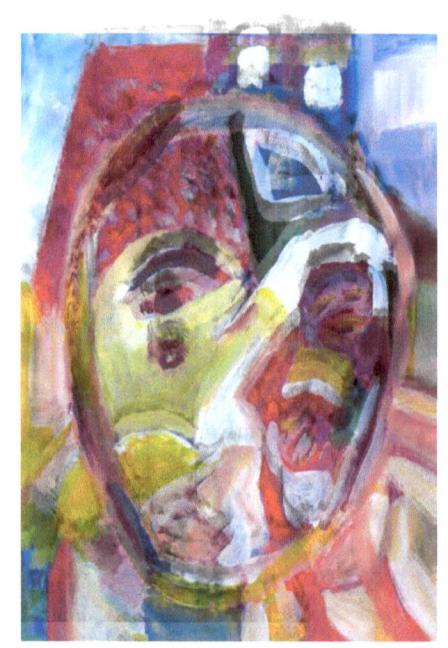

Rodica told me her story.

After her mother turned off the light in her room, she would read by the light of a street lamp.
For this, she would sit on the windowsill of her room window.

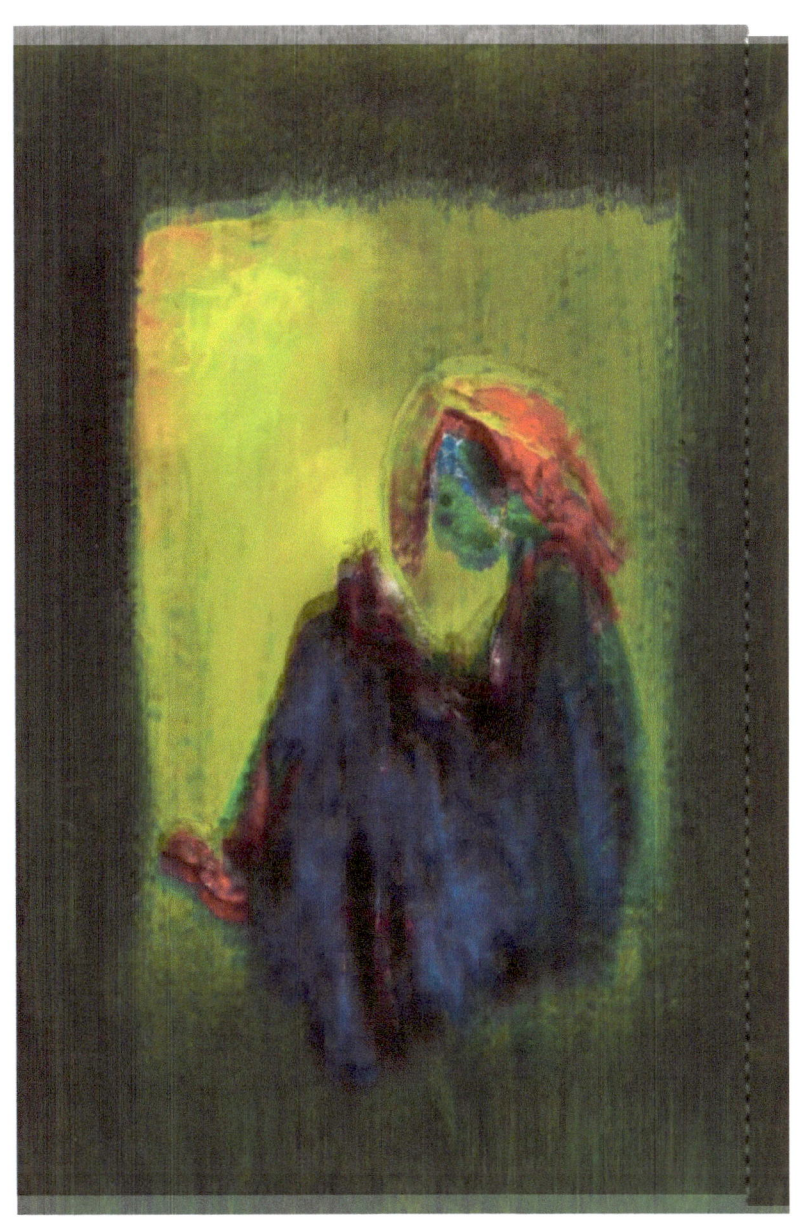

Digital Transformations (pre-2014) and facing the computer

When playing with a computer, many things can happen. Below are the results of my first attempts at using an application to produce pictures on a computer screen. As I did not have the resources, my only helper was always a small mouse. I also used several of my one minute acrylic paintings and next page, photographs.

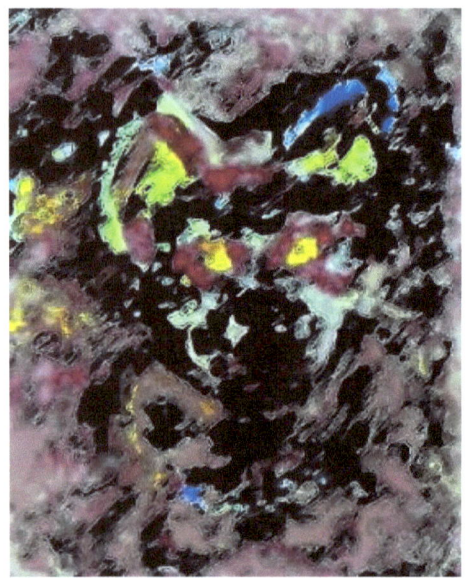

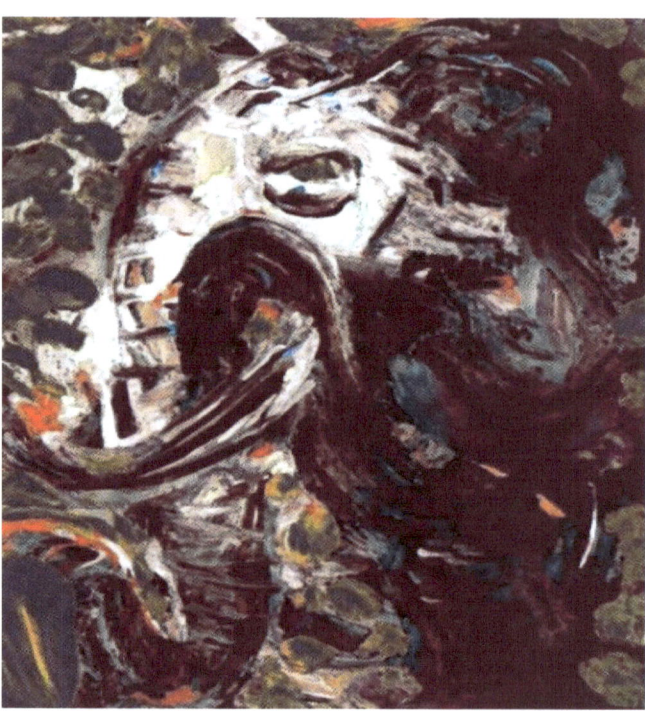

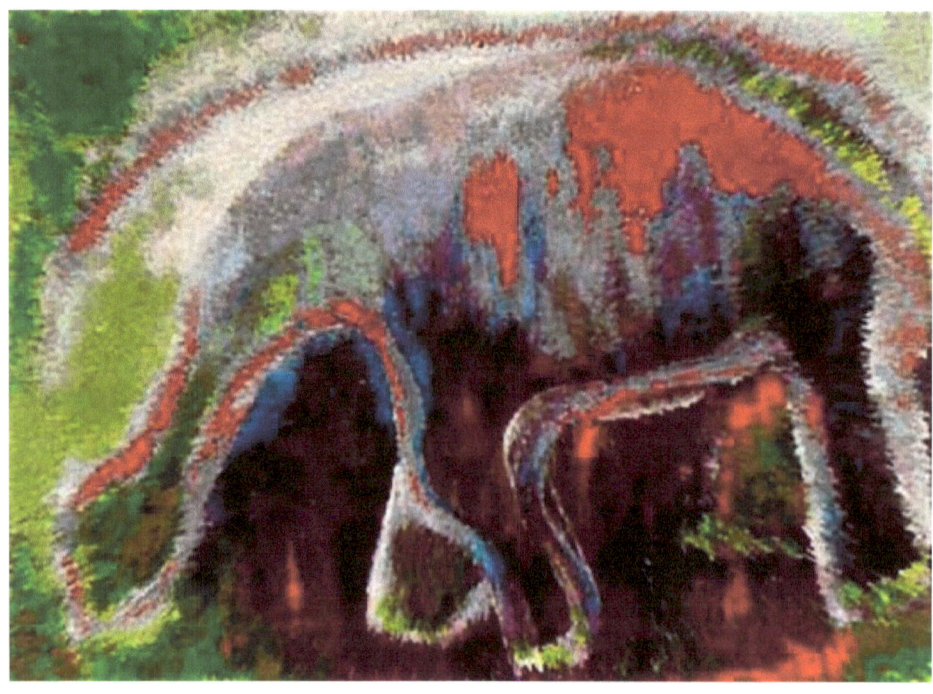

Interesting. I've never really been into photo manipulation, but here are two examples.
Blitz and Churchill with his grandchildren at the window of a small shack,
with the same Blitz soldier standing guard outside.

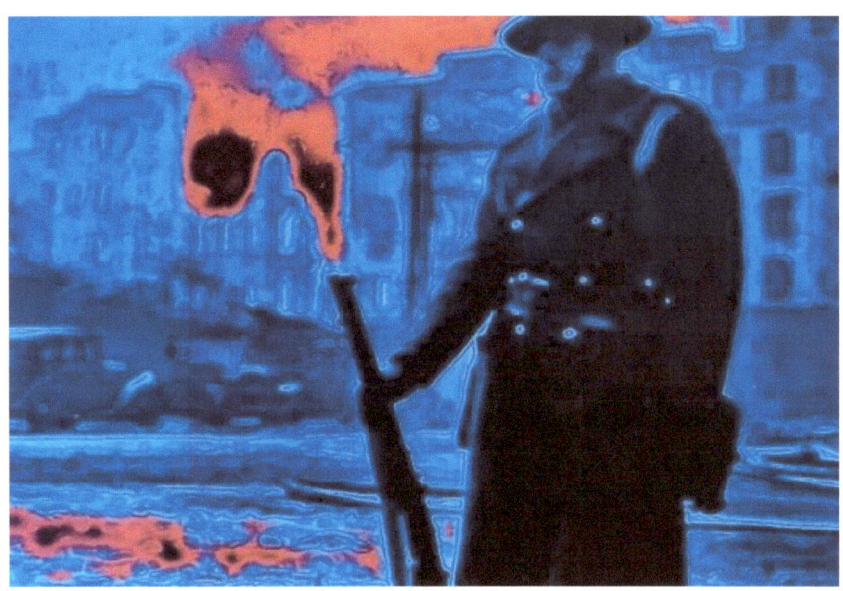

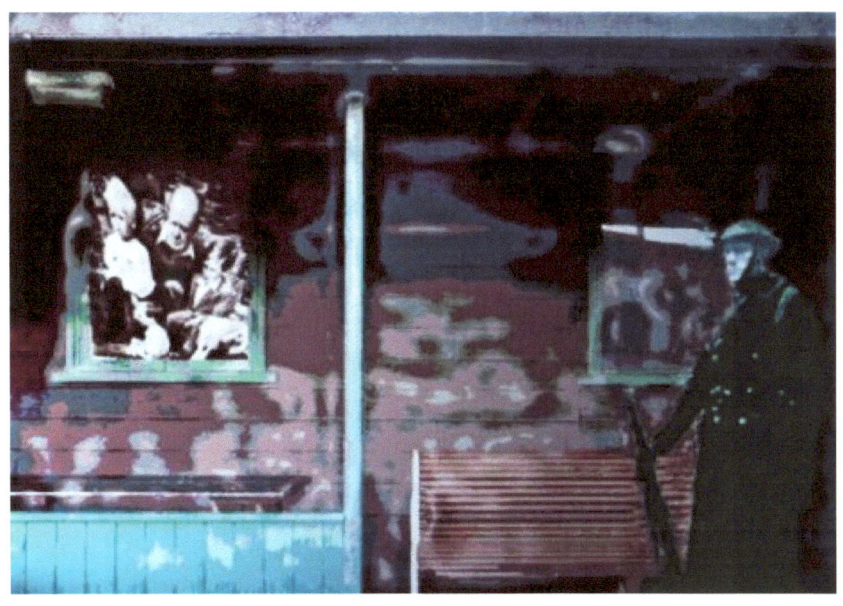

Gayton Road
Gayton Road

Learning and discovering.
Learning and discovering.

The digital mix, or the beginning.
The digital mix, or the beginning.

*
*

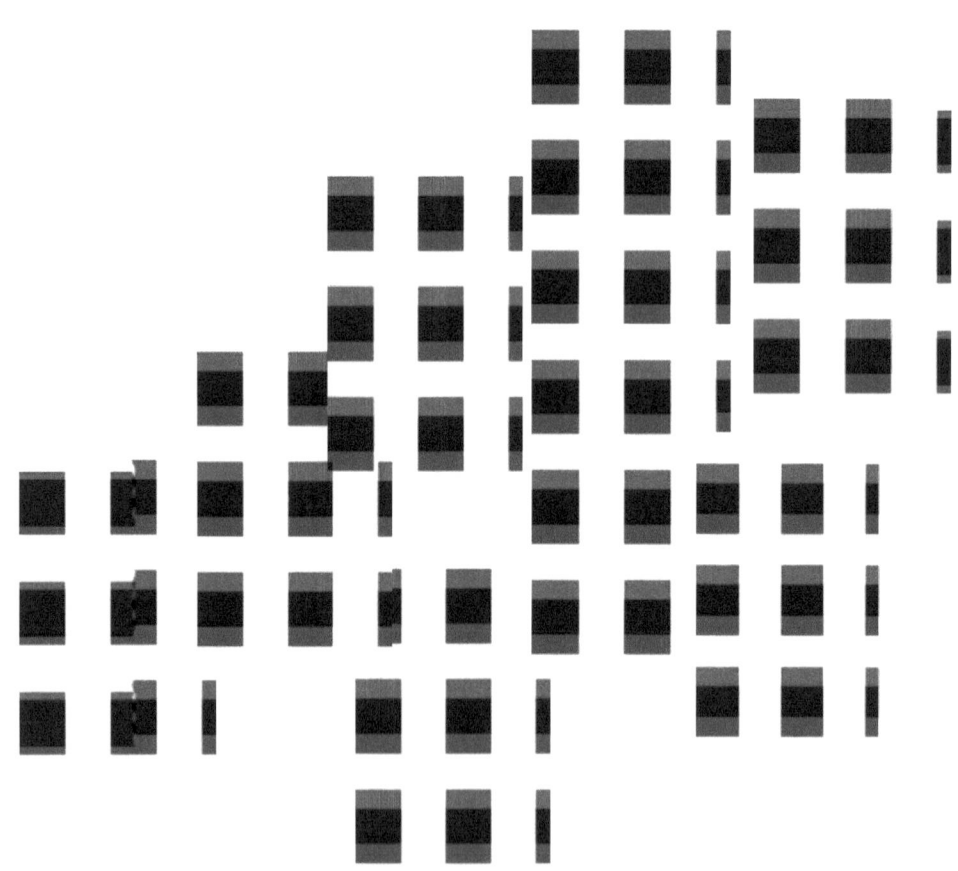

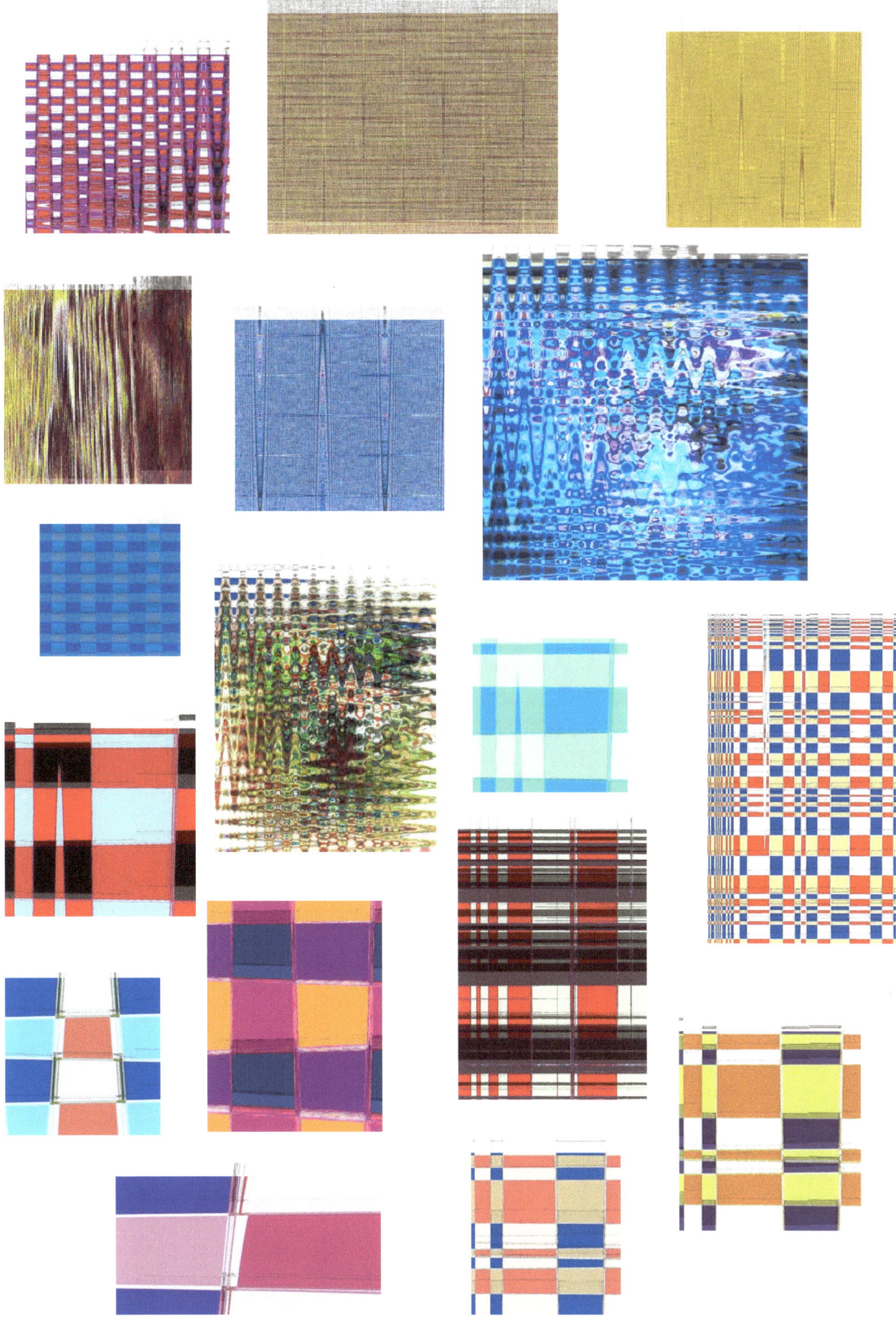

2012

Each little square contains a photo.

It seems to me that many people - meaning, artists - have had this same idea in many parts of the world.

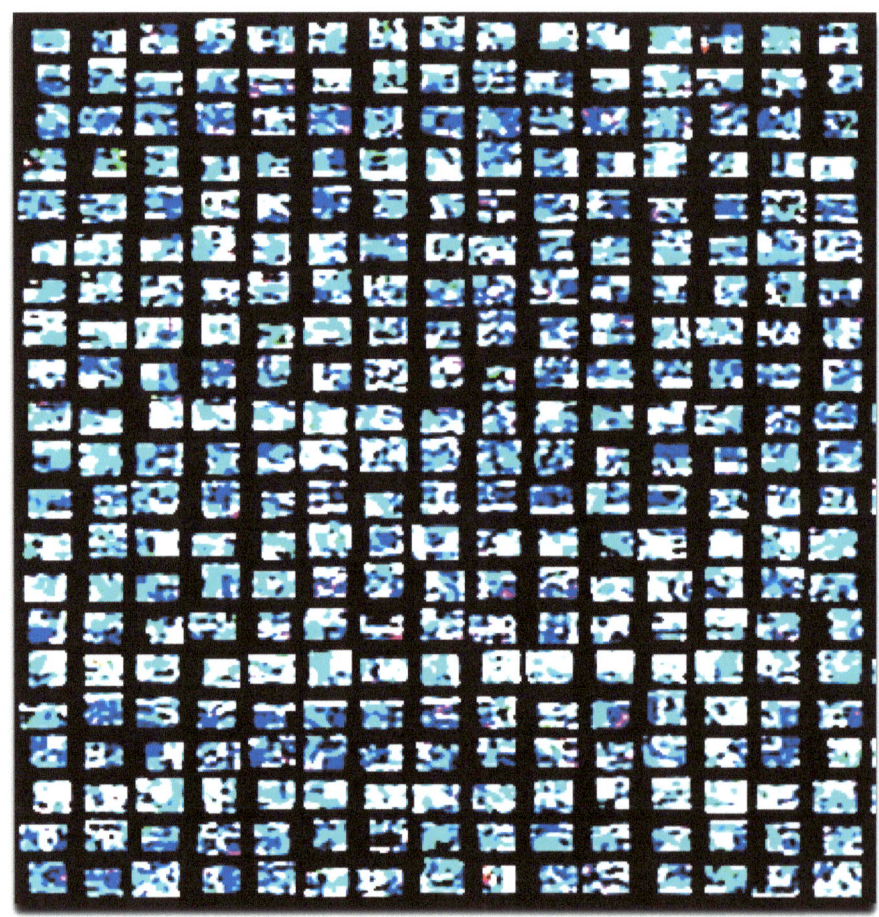

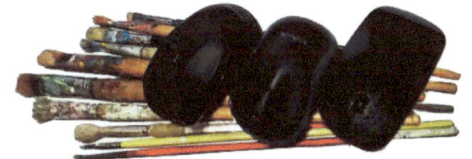

Thomas Hewelett House, again.

As an amateur painter with no more wall space for my work and no serious commitment to the craft, I ended up using a computer to occupy my time. Most of the work I did was very simple, involving copy and paste and a little digital painting. All done with the mouse; nothing special. The Exotis are my cosmic trade mark Aliens part of many little stories. Below are some book covers I have produced. Most covers and books were translated into Portuguese:

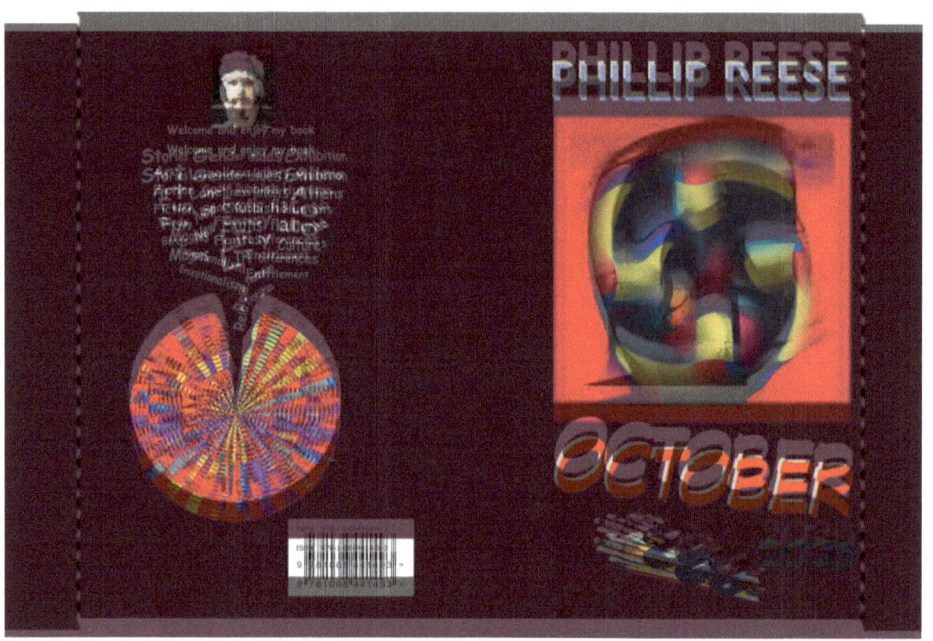

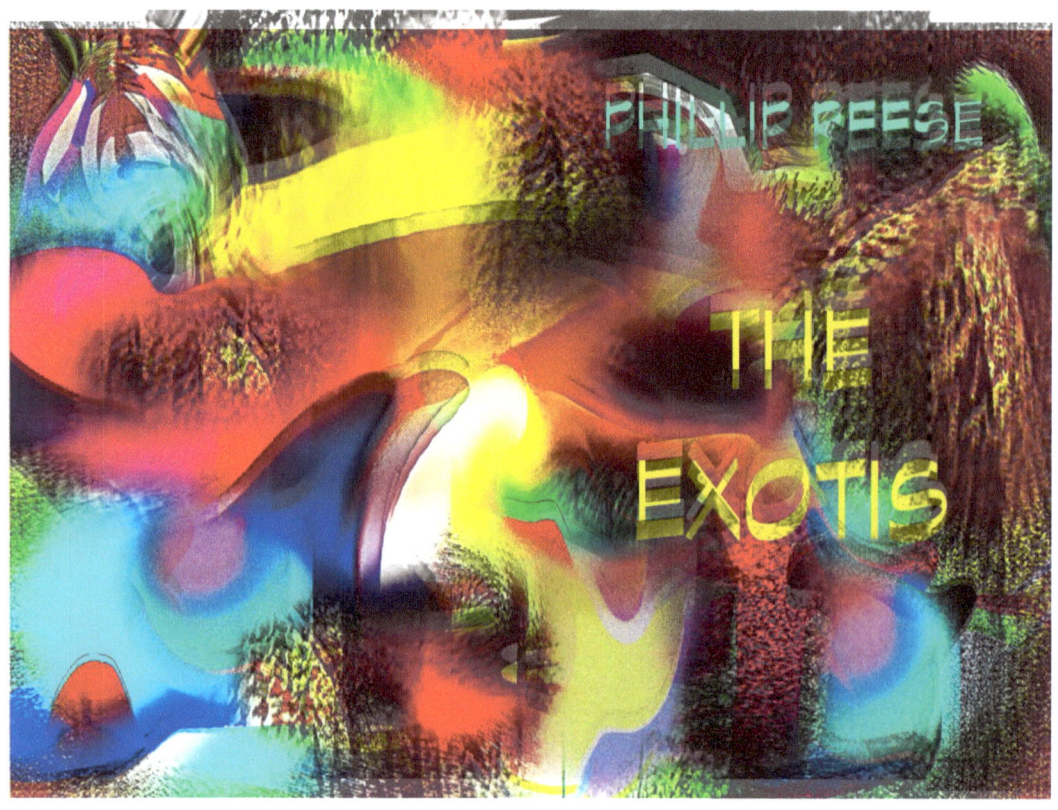

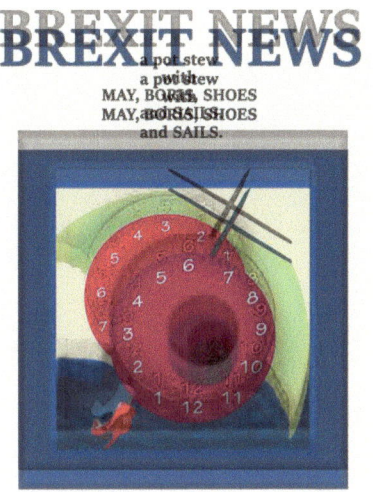

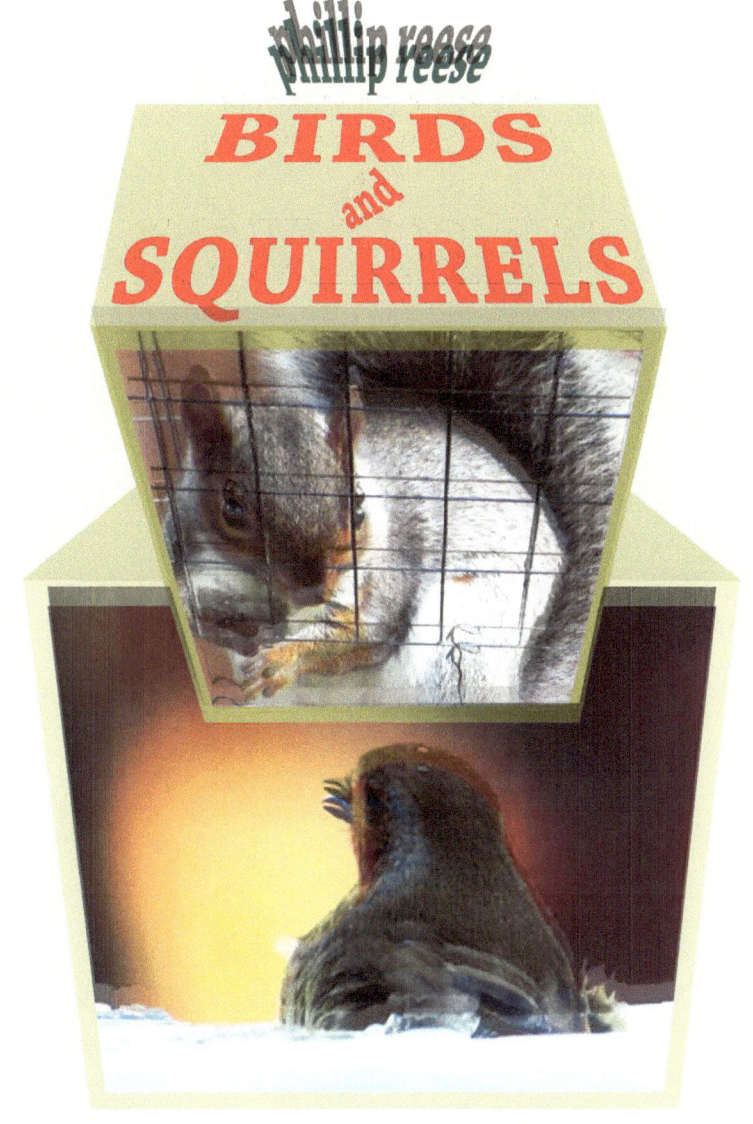

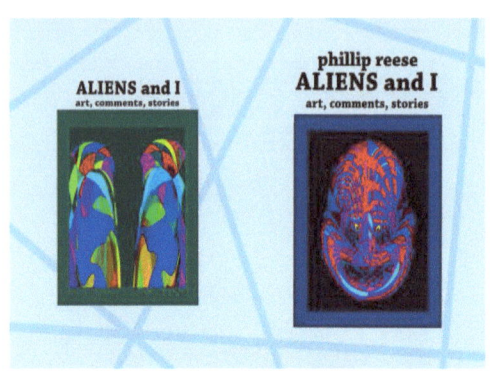

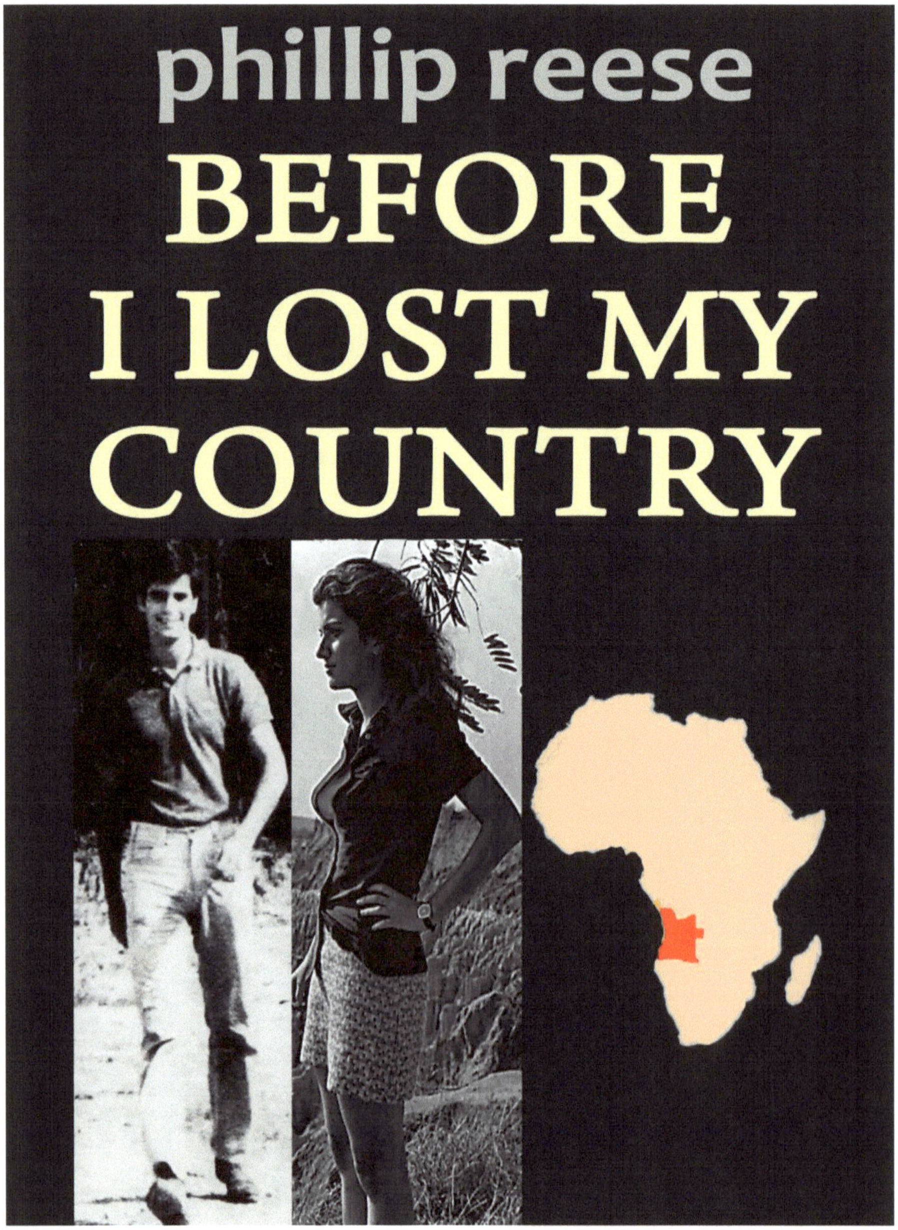

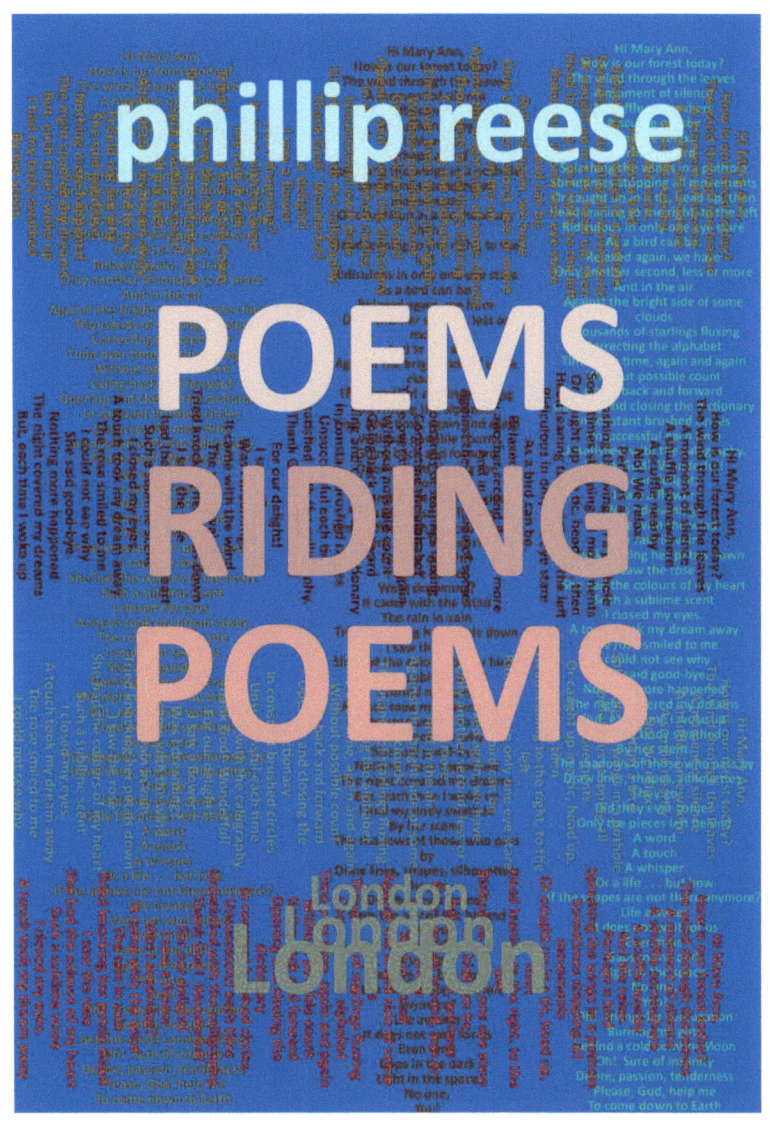
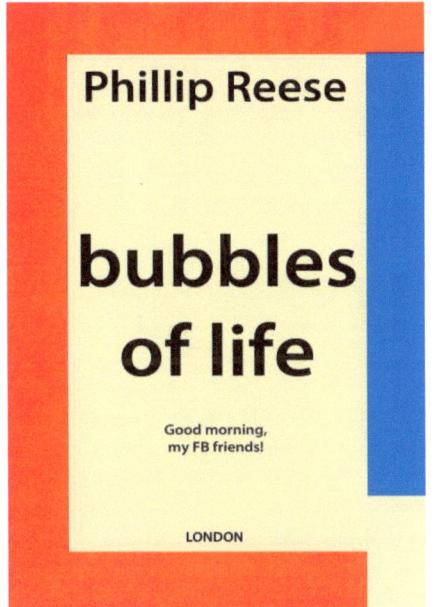
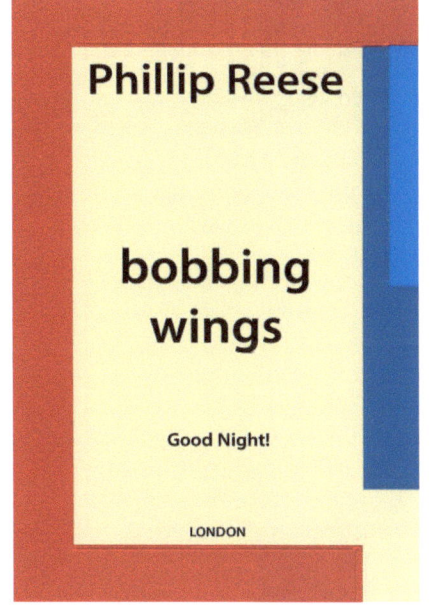

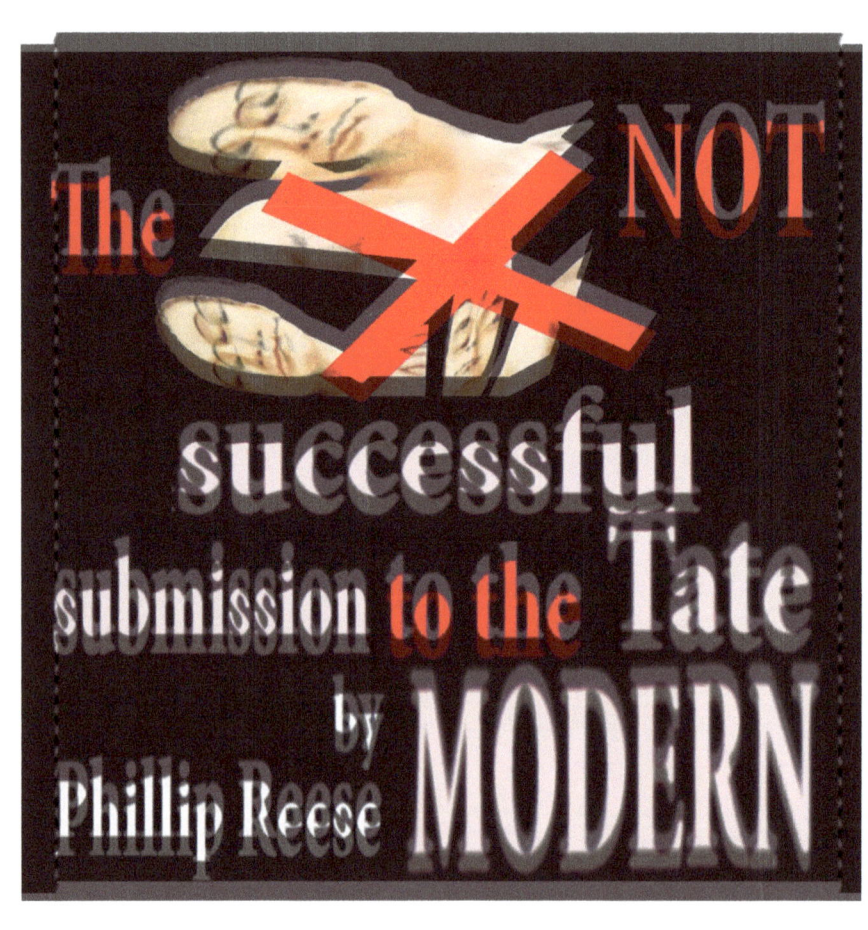

This book is being revised at the moment

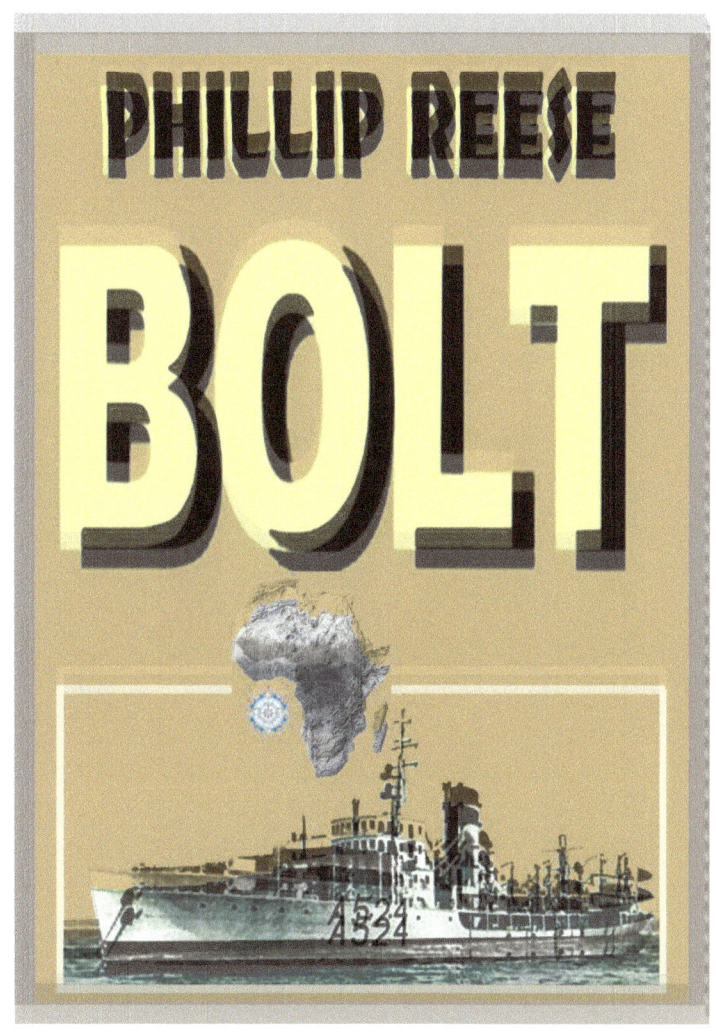

Part II

Next are a few little pieces of art out
of the hundreds I did,
some of which are recent (2026).

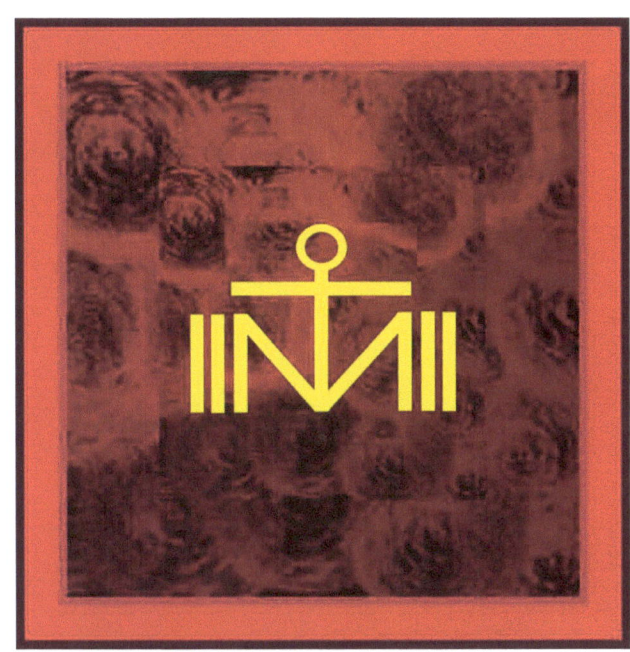
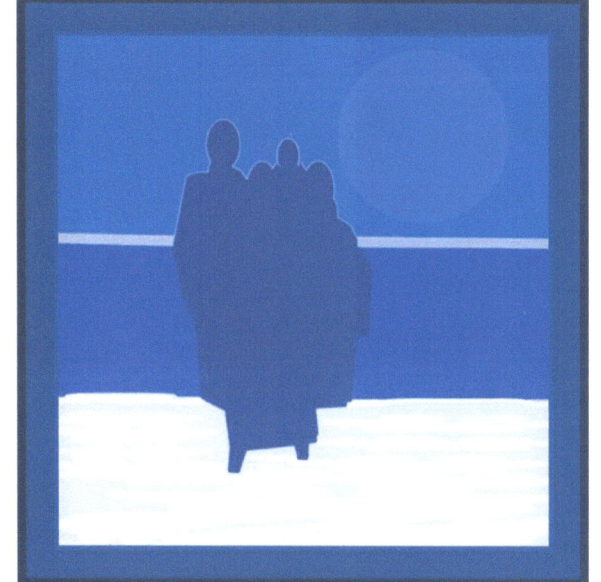
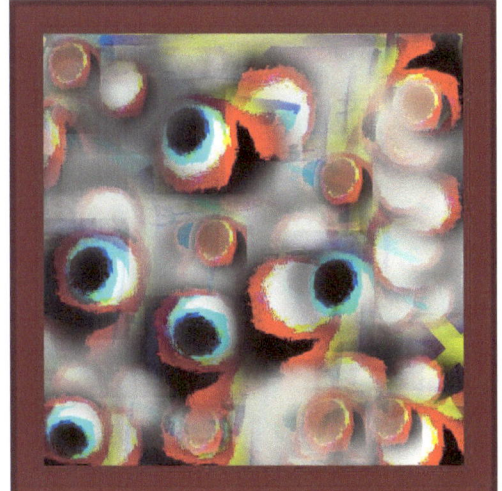
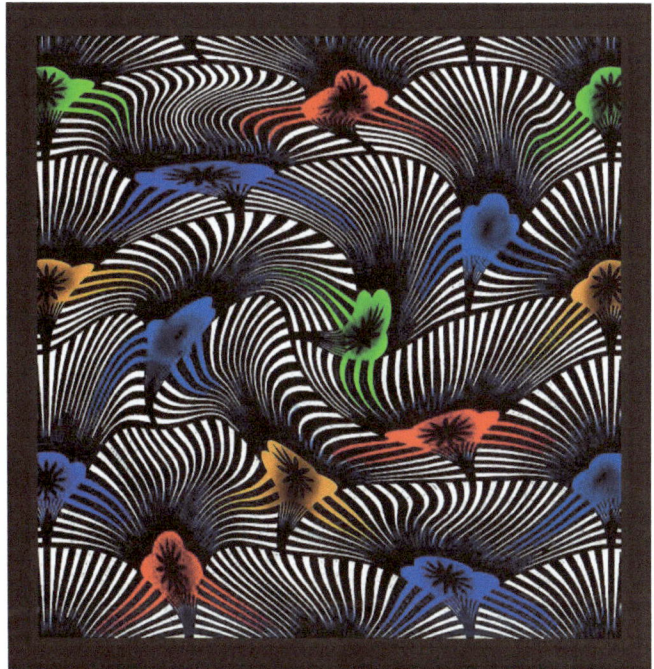
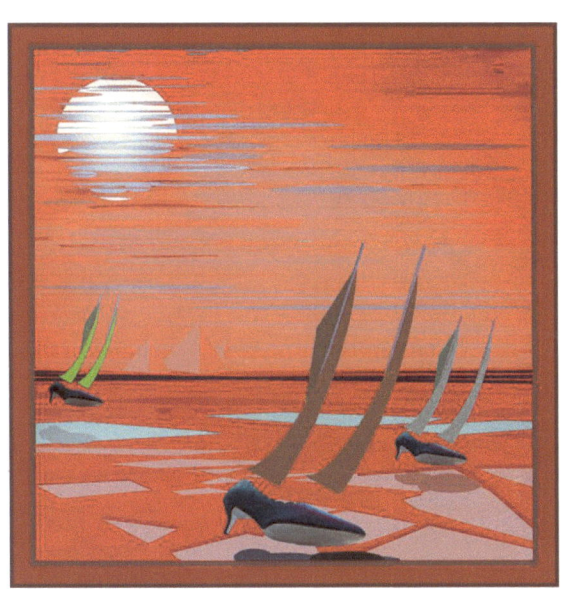

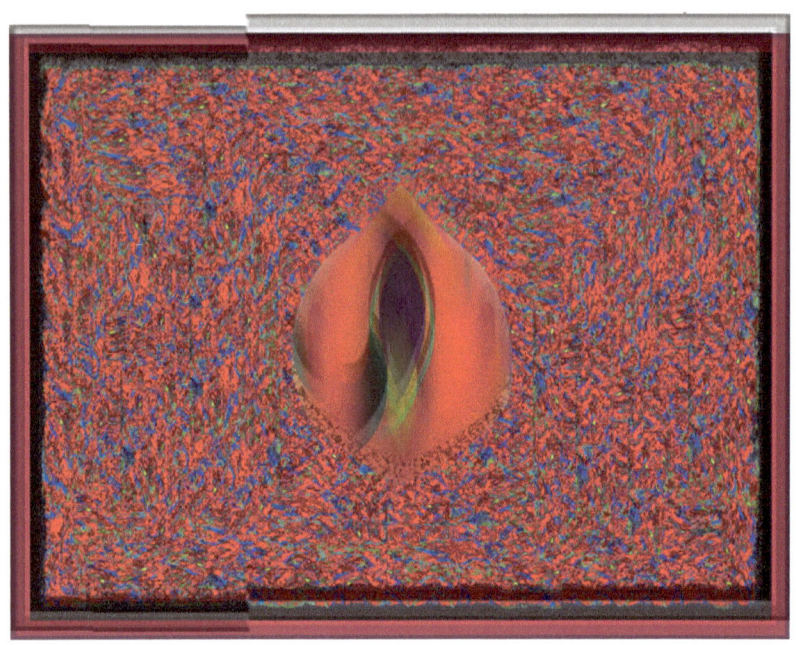
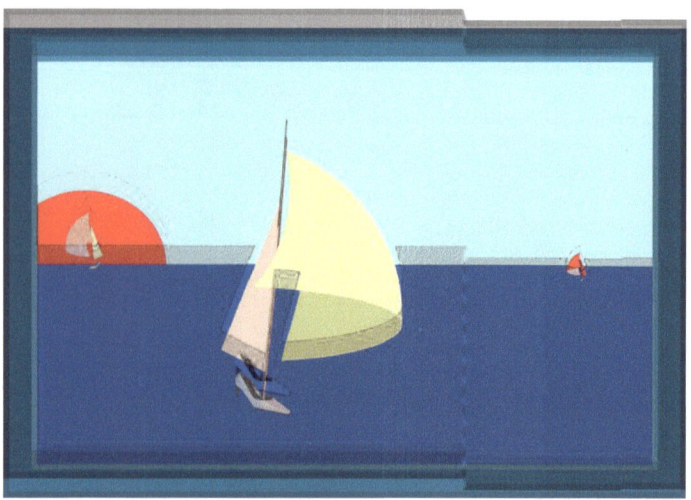
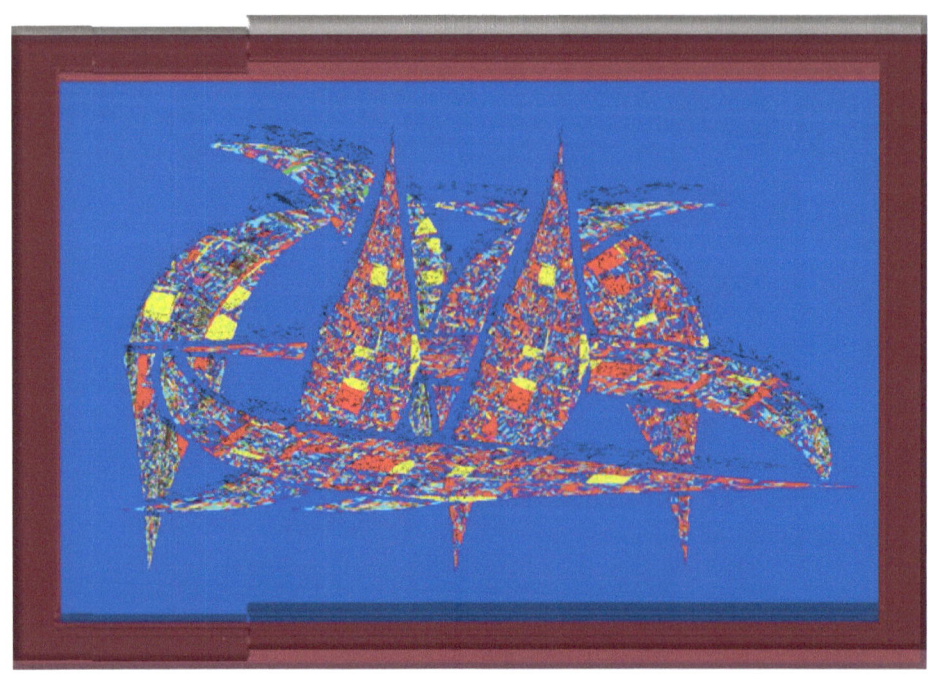

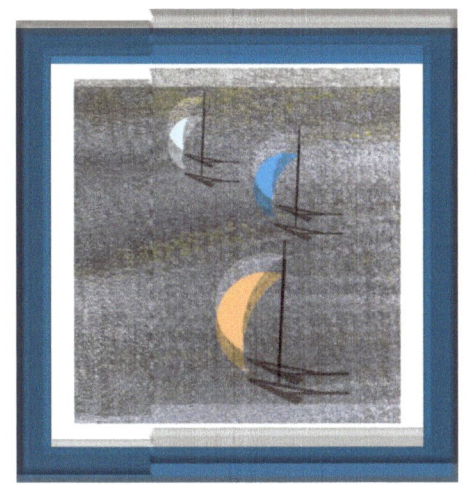
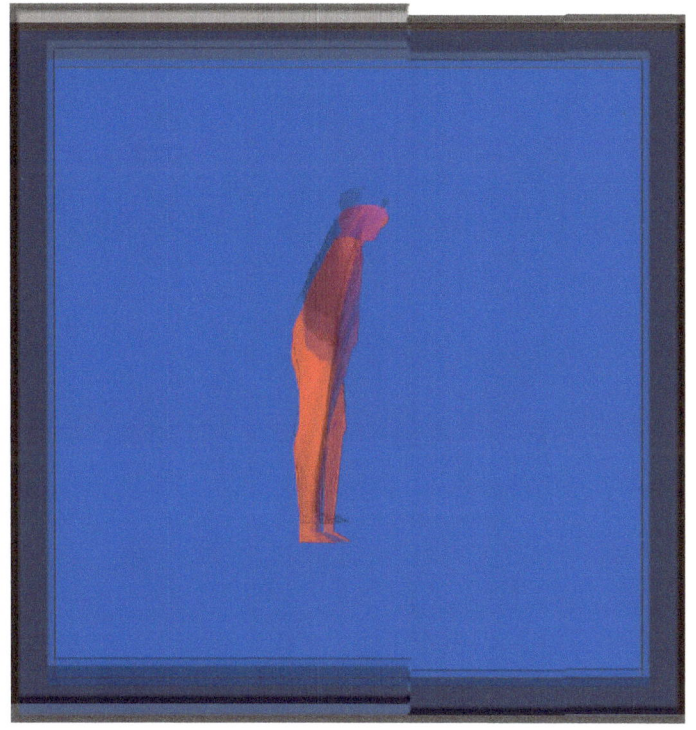
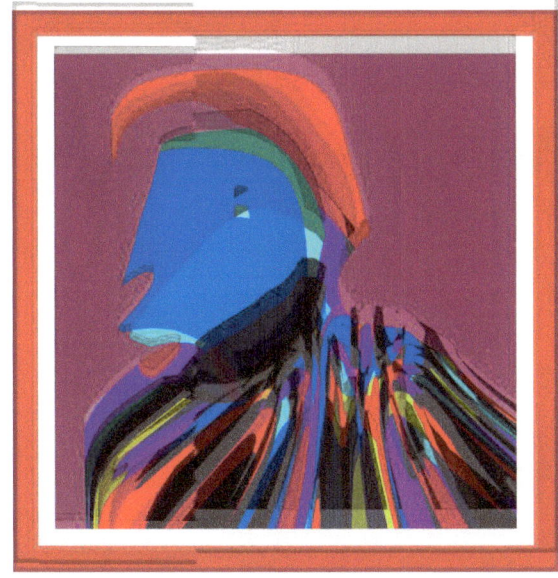
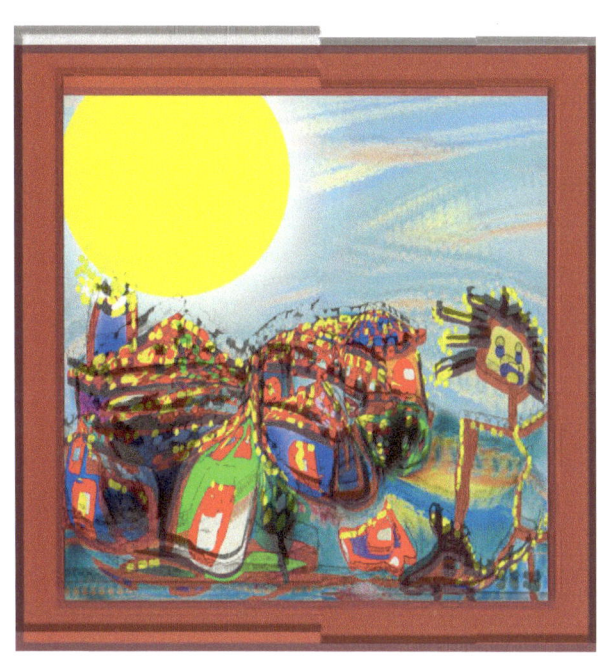

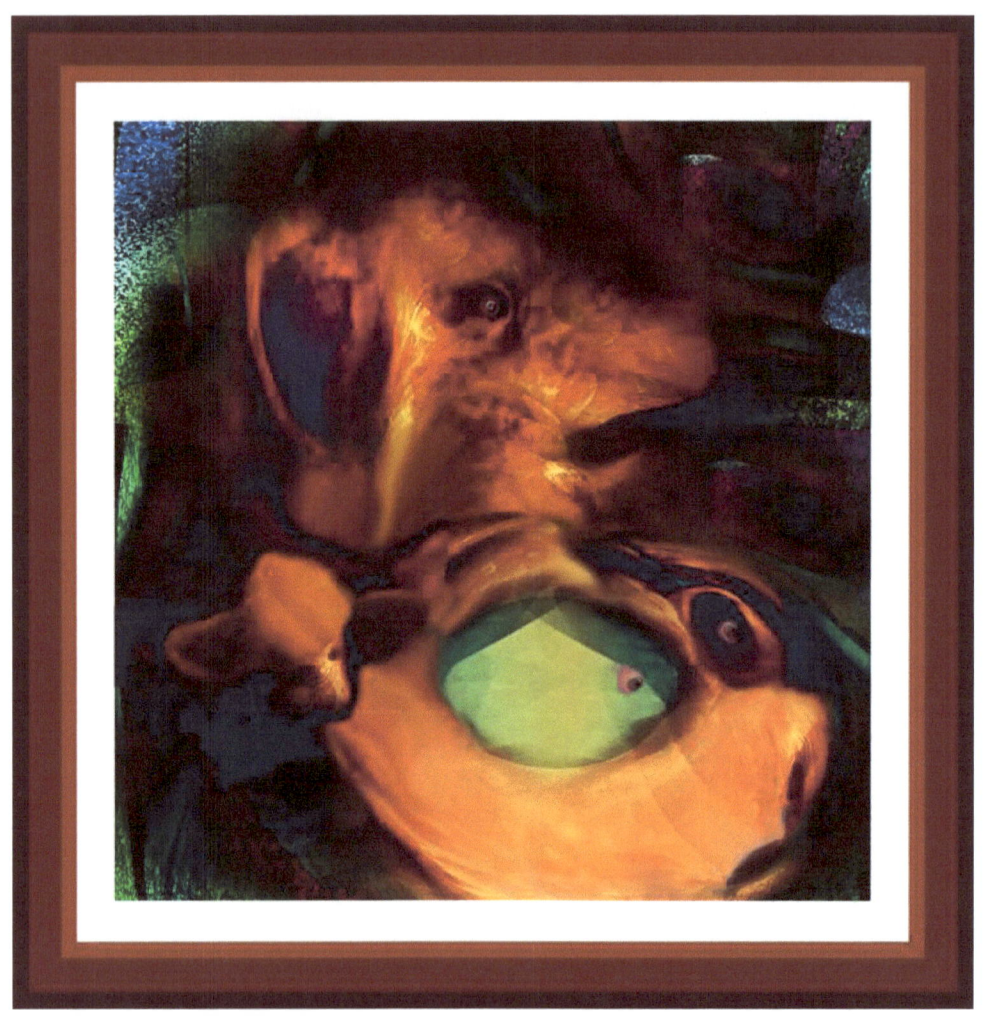

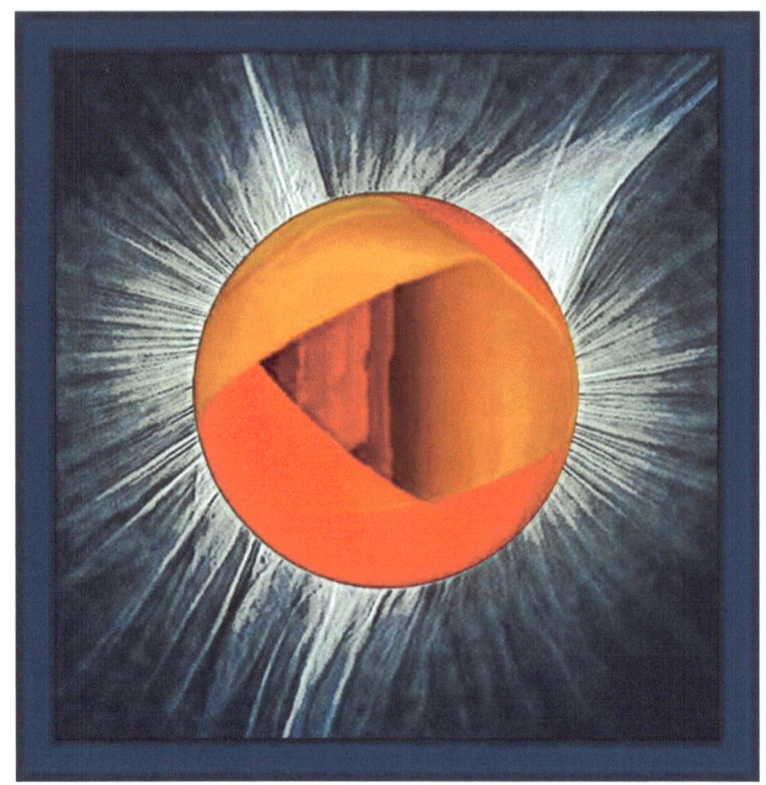

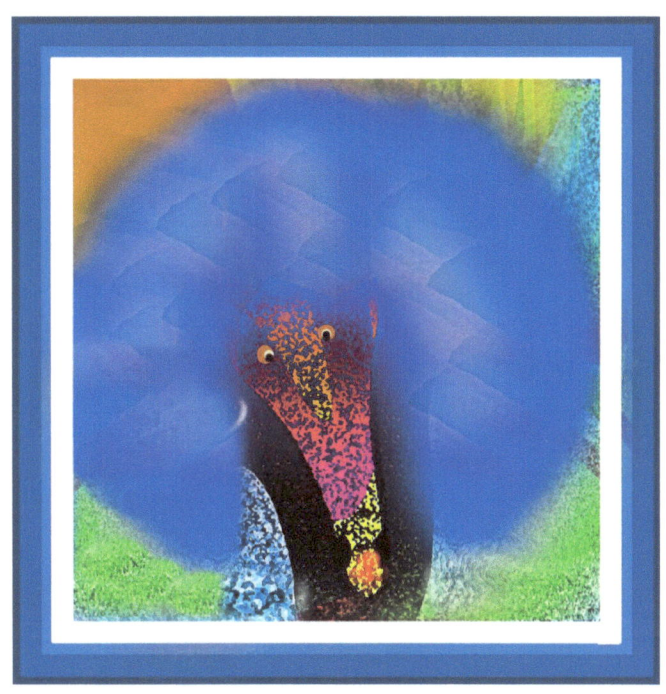

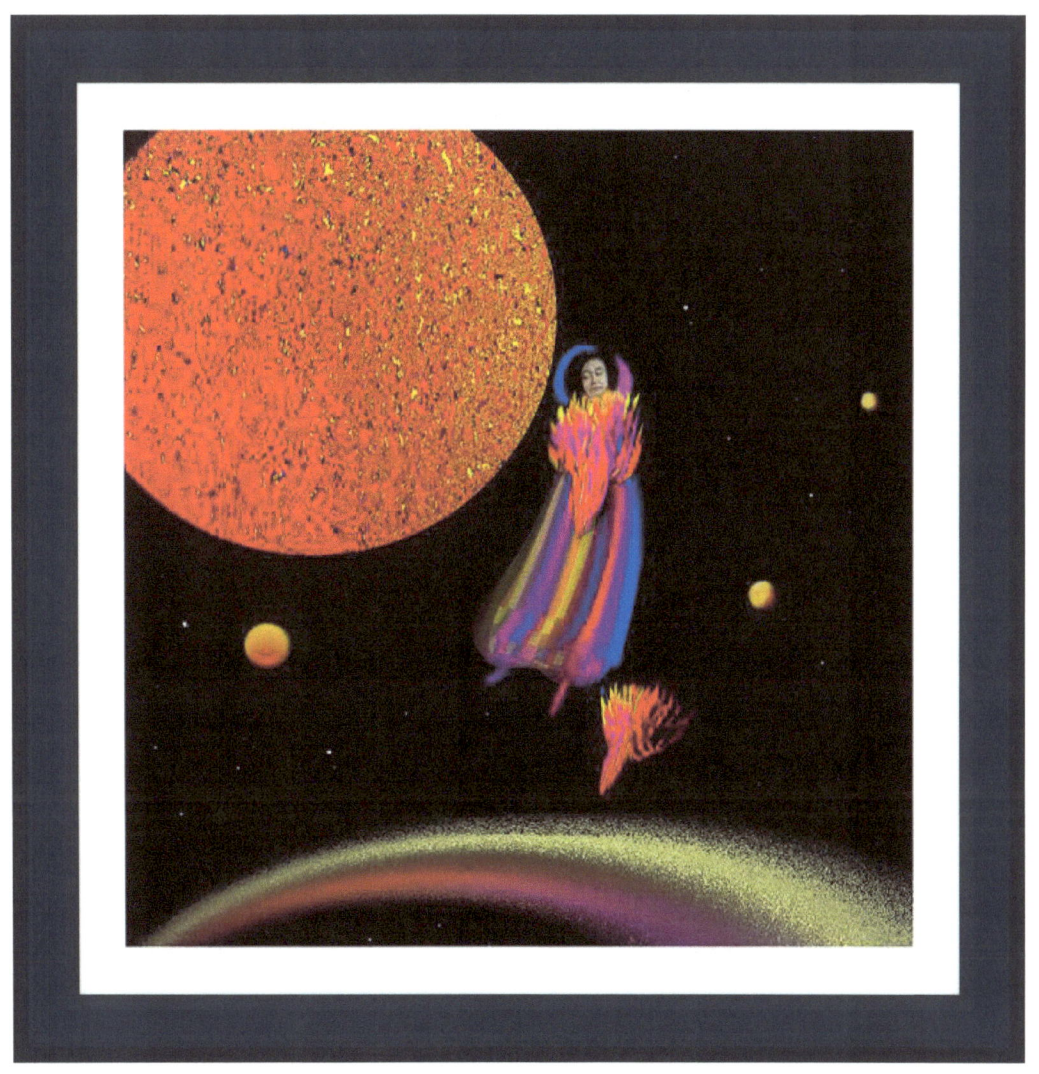

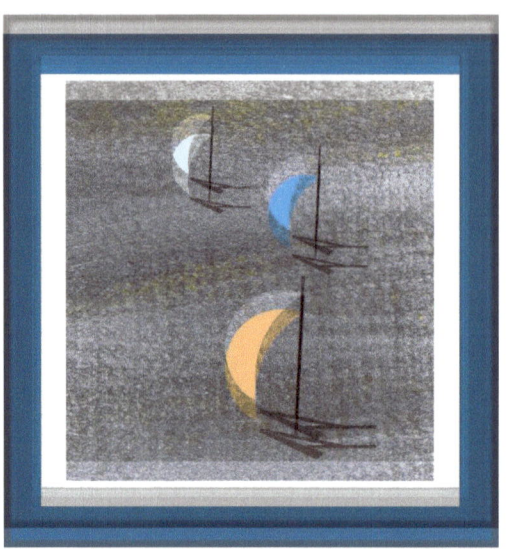
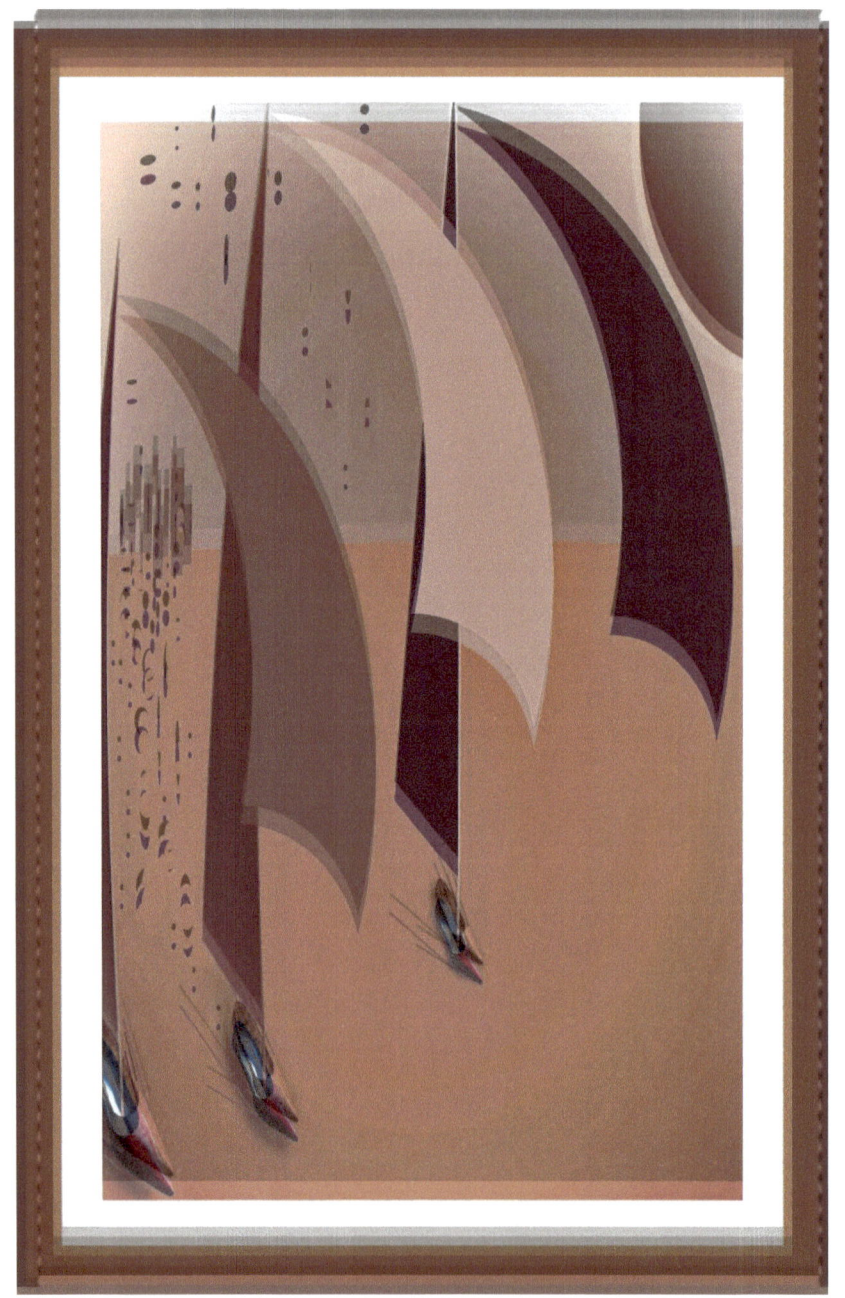

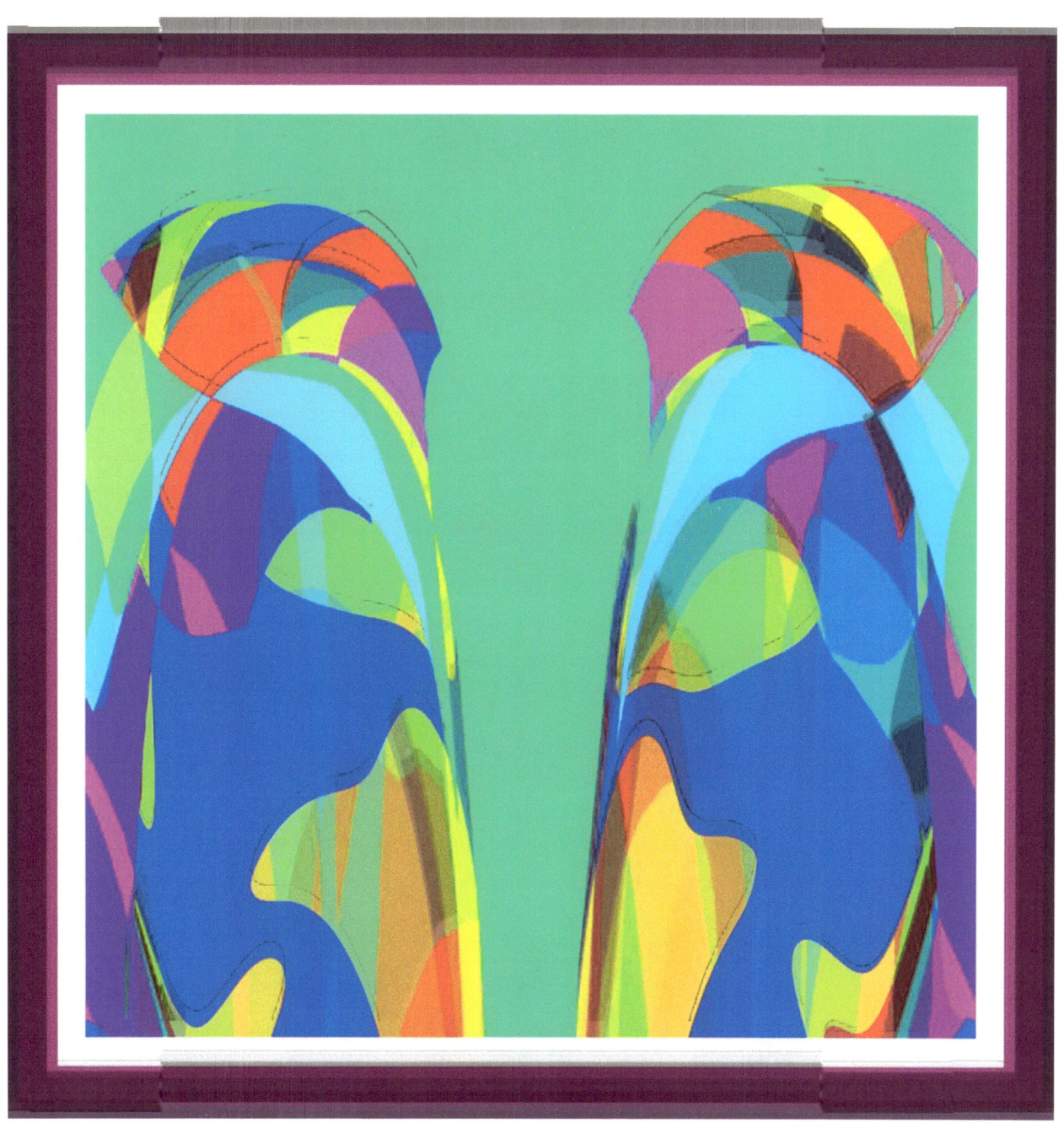

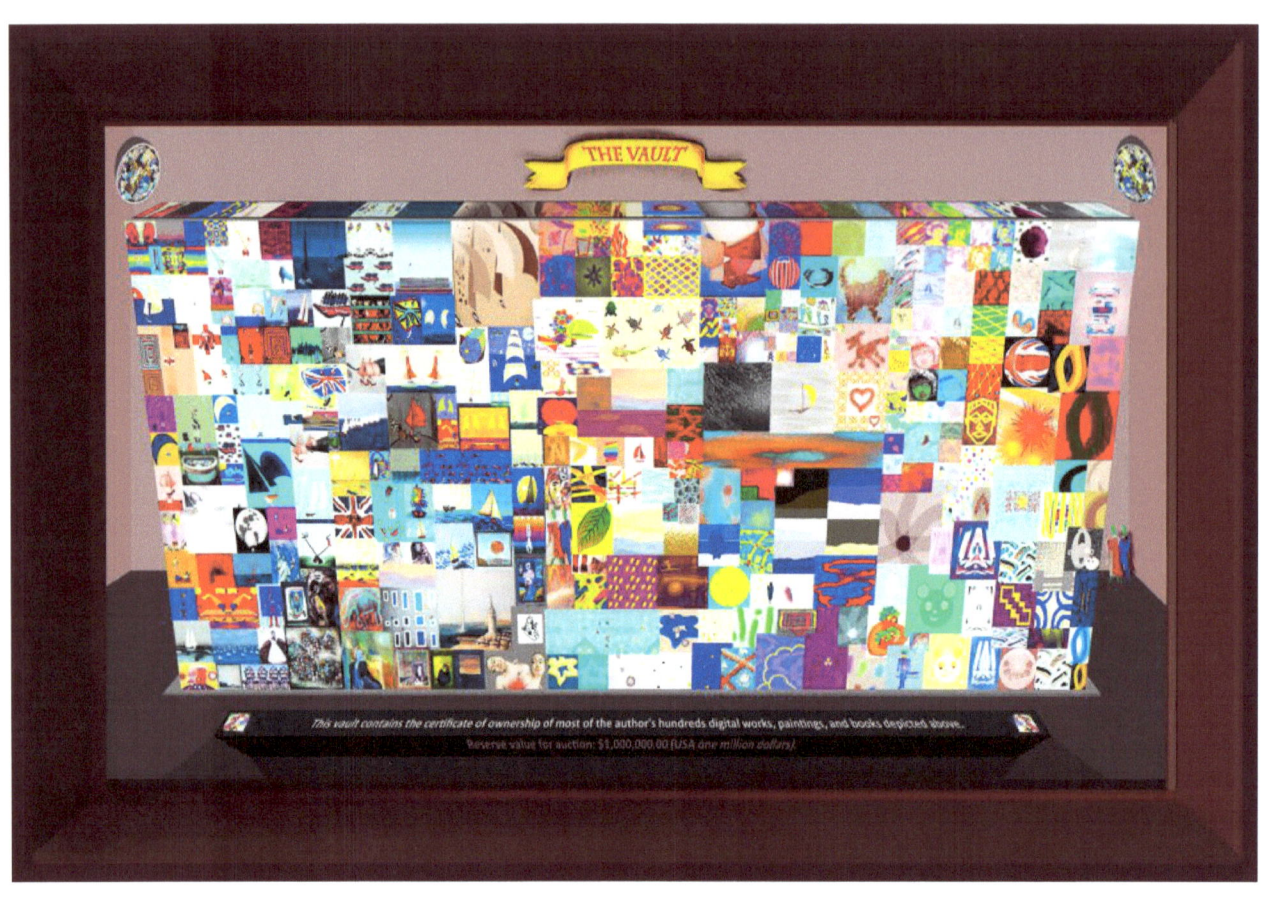

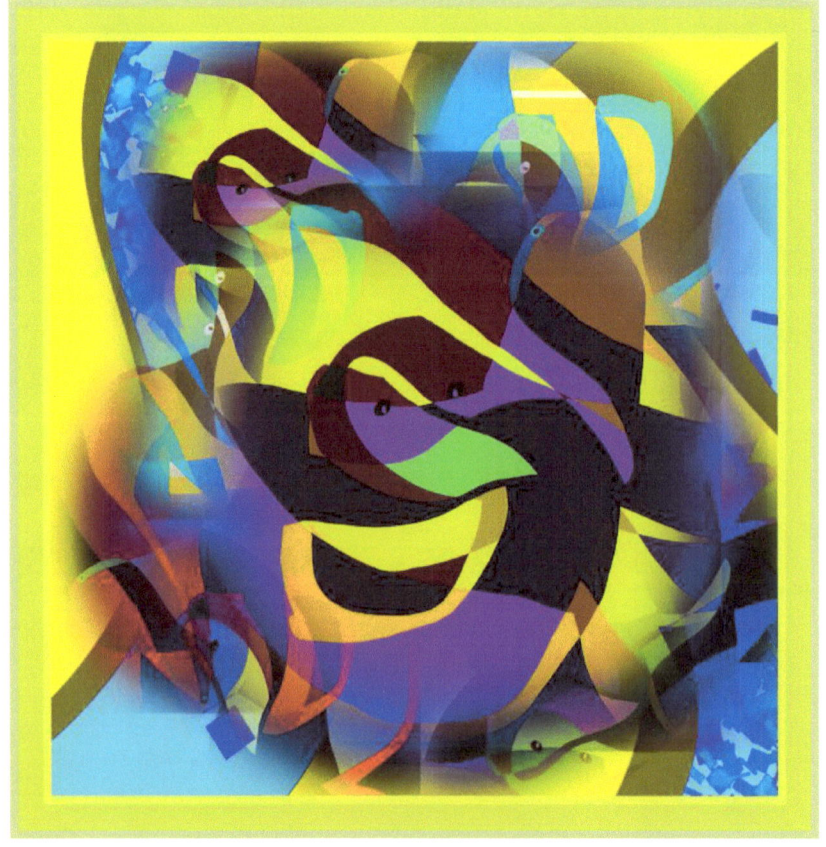

www.ingramcontent.com/pod-product-compliance
Lightning Source LLC
Chambersburg PA
CBHW051922210526
45473CB00006B/2107